Seven Come Eleven

Seven Come Eleven

How to Stop Depression and Start Living

H. George Arsenault

iUniverse, Inc.
New York   Lincoln   Shanghai

Seven Come Eleven
How to Stop Depression and Start Living

iUniverse books may be ordered through booksellers or by contacting:

iUniverse
2021 Pine Lake Road, Suite 100
Lincoln, NE 68512
www.iuniverse.com
1-800-Authors (1-800-288-4677)

Because of the dynamic nature of the Internet, any Web addresses
or links contained in this book may have changed
since publication and may no longer be valid.

The views expressed in this work are solely those of the author and do
not necessarily reflect the views of the publisher, and the publisher hereby
disclaims any responsibility for them.

ISBN: 978-0-595-45597-3 (pbk)
ISBN: 978-0-595-89898-5 (ebk)

Printed in the United States of America

This book is the reporting of two autobiography books in the life and times of H. George Arsenault. It starts with Book I—"My Blue Heaven" and concludes with Book II—"One Plus One Equals Nineteen" as the author gives his reasons in explanation of why a single man with seven young children would marry a single women with ten young children. The title "Seven Come Eleven" ends with the single man's seven dependents from Book I "My Blue Heaven" and he adds ten more children plus a wife making eleven more dependents with Book II "One Plus One Equals Nineteen."

Contents

Book II: One Plus One Equals Nineteen

List of Photos and Illustration

BOOK I

MY BLUE HEAVEN

This book is dedicated to Margaret Elizabeth Foley, my loving wife of twelve years, and my seven children, Mary Ann, Patrick Joseph, Margaret Elizabeth, Robert Ernest, Mark Anthony, Aileen Therese, and Janet Frances, for their unfailing love and support before and after their mother died on May 26, 1964.

FOREWORD

A Book Report on "My Blue Heaven" by William X. Kienzle, Author of "The Rosary Murders" made into a movie of the same name and author of 24 Mystery Novels.

I found "My Blue Heaven" compelling. Once more truth is more unexpected than fiction. The reader knows how this story must end. But hopes against hope that the inevitable will somehow be derailed. "My Blue Heaven" is a moving experience.

PREFACE

Much like the Shakespearean tragedy, Hamlet, tells the story of how fate, *with the slings and arrows of outrageous fortune*, deals a man a devastating blow, destroying his status quo, and how he confronts it. *My Blue Heaven* is a true story in like manner. In the *preface* of my first published book *One Plus One Equals Nineteen*, I mentioned this paradox.

I discovered that blue can not only mean happiness, like *blue skies* or the *blue bird of happiness* or *blue bird hill* as in the movie *Going My Way*, but sometimes it can also mean sadness, similar to *singing the blues* in our jazz age. How to cope with these events that fate presents us with from time to time is something that every one of us must learn in order to avoid chronic depression. Searching for answers, I turned to the bible with its reference to faith, hope and charity. I also took a college course in Philosophy and reading the philosophical wisdom of sages of the past, I found the support I needed. I learned I could pray for faith and always have hope for charity. I became an optimist.

Therefore, I have always alleged to be an optimist. I remember reading this axiom: *as you wander on through life, whatever is your goal, keep your eye upon the doughnut and not upon the hole.*—This became my motto. *The glass isn't half empty—it's half full!*

ACKNOWLEDGMENTS

The renowned mystery writer, William X. Kienzle, who has written over twenty mystery novels, including the *Rosary Murders* that was made into a movie of the same name, is an old Holy Redeemer School classmate of mine. Bill's wife, Javan, a retired proofreader and editor from the Detroit Free Press, reviewed my original manuscript, which was written into two major parts combined and called *Seven Come Eleven* as one manuscript. As you may have read in my prior book, *One Plus One Equals Nineteen*, I was fortunate to obtain their astute counseling.

Javan read my manuscript and made many corrections suggesting that I really had two books. It became clear to me, that because of the total distinction and uniqueness of the two parts, I really had two stories that could not be told together as one book. Bill and Javan encouraged me to pursue its publication. Neal Shine, retired publisher of the Detroit Free Press and one of Michigan's most respected journalists, who is a neighbor of mine, also encouraged me to publish this autobiography.

Having been rejected by many publishers and at Bill Kienzle's suggestion, I solicited Berl Falbaum, an author and professional public relations specialist, former reporter for The Detroit News, teacher at two state universities, to assist me in the final proof reading of my manuscript in preparation for self publication. Berl suggested that I concentrate on seventeen and thus, "*One Plus One Equals Nineteen*" preceded "My Blue Heaven" book. "1+1=19" is a happy lighthearted chronicle that tells the story of how one widow and one widower merged in a joint venture of marriage to raise seventeen children. It relates all the problems and how they were solved.

Now, "My Blue Heaven" is the beginning or what came before that story. "My Blue Heaven" has a happy ending with "1+1=19" book.

I especially wish to acknowledge my debt to Delores Ann Shmina McMillan Arsenault, my wife of "1+1=19," for her devoted love and support in helping me with my writing efforts, by proofreading, critiquing, and correcting both books: *One Plus One Equals Nineteen* and now, *"My Blue Heaven."*

INTRODUCTION

Ulysses S. Grant in the preface of his **Personal Memoirs of U.S. Grant** stated, *"Man proposes and God disposes."* I have the same opinion. There are many important events in our lives that are not in our plans nor brought about by their own choice. God or fate has a way of writing our history in such a manner that seems to go beyond our thoughts and expectations. Sometimes the events in our lives exceed the best fiction or prophecy of anyone's imagination. So it was in my day.

I

MY PHILOSOPHY

> *There are more things in heaven and earth, Horatio,*
>
> *Than are dreamed of in your*
> *philosophy.—Shakespeare.*

"What's your philosophy for life?" A certain professor of philosophy was asking us. "Your homework is to write a short paper stating your philosophy for life. Something simple," he said, "that would identify what you believe and what were your rules and values for living the good life." I remember that that 'short paper' was not simple but a rather difficult task.

Socrates talked about "defining your terms" before he could discuss anything. We need to know what is meant by *philosophy* before we can write our *philosophy for life*. Socrates defined *philosophy* as the pursuit of wisdom and one who seeks knowledge or a seeker of the truth. Webster defines *philosophy of life* as "… an attitude towards life and the purpose of life." With this, I attempted to define my most general beliefs, concepts, and attitudes for my life in the following dissertation.

From my youth, I always wanted to live honorably. I felt that a person who lives honorably would never cheat, never lie, never steal, and never waiver from the straight and narrow path of fairness. He will know the difference between right and wrong and always choose right. His reward will be a good life and eternal happiness. I thought of myself as a knight in shining armor, riding a white horse and ready to slay the evil dragon for his beautiful princess. The dragon was sin and therefore, like Tom Sawyer told his aunt when she asked him what the preacher said about sin, he answered, "He's agin it!" *(Sic)* And so was I. This is my philosophy.

As time went on, I found that the challenge for me in later years was to pass this sense of moral purpose and values on to my children so, then, hopefully, they could enjoy the happiness and rewards of a life well spent. The feelings and problems that spiritual impoverishment can lead to depression and unrelenting sadness. This is something every one of us sometimes experience. I was taught at an early age to trust in God and never lose hope. I was happy that I had been given faith and could look to God for guidance, strength and support.

Without this philosophy and religion, I don't know how I could have faced the life that was waiting for me in the near future. I was told that nothing was impossible with the help and guidance of God and that one could easily attain the blue heaven of their dreams if they only had faith in God.

A Frenchman, named Antoine de Rivarol, over two hundred years ago stated, It *is easy for men to write and talk like philosophers, but to act with wisdom, there's the rub!* Wisdom—now—there's the rub! I remember starting to pray for wisdom when my father died. I was nine years old and wondered why my dad had died. I worried about my mother having enough money to continue living in our house. Luckily, my dad had paid cash for the house.

After my father died, the teaching nuns in my Catholic school told me to pray for the wisdom to understand God's plan. So, at nine years old, I added a prayer for wisdom every night before I went to bed. I thought that I could solve all my problems easily and successfully and the world would be mine if only God would grant me wisdom.

From the beginning, my mother taught my brother, sister and I to say our prayers on our knees every night before we went to bed. I remember that we would always include: "God bless mother, dad and my brother and sister, etc." With the etcetera, we would include a bunch of other people. At nine years old, as a third grader, I was still praying every night. In fact, we were taught to say night prayers and morning prayers. It was many years later that this practice changed. As I was growing up, in high school, I decided that you need not be on your knees to pray and you don't have to wait for bedtime or morning.

II

IN THE BEGINNING

> *The Book of Life begins with a man and woman in a garden.*
>
> *It ends with Revelations.—Oscar Wilde.*

The year was 1671 when Pierre, a navigator on a French sailing ship called "L'Oranger" sailed out of La Rochelle, France and headed west for the new world. He was the first Arsenault to arrive in the North American continent. Born in 1650, at Rochefort, a small village near the central west coast of France. Pierre, at the age of 21, landed at Port Royal, Acadia in what is now called Nova Scotia, Canada.

Nine generations later, on the 30th of September 1927, I was born. This was the month that Charles Lindbergh first published his new book recounting his solo flight over the Atlantic of the prior May when Paris had hailed him the *Lone Eagle*. He called his book "We" because—as he stated in his book—his lonely flight could not have happen without the support of many associates

It was a good year. The stock market was rising higher and higher, making more and more of its speculators rich. Babe Ruth set a new record with his 60th home run of the season and the Yankees beat the Pirates for the World Series. The first talking picture, *The Jazz Singer* starring Al Jolson, was released.

The *Teapot Dome scandal* caused the Supreme Court to rule that the Navy oil land leases in Wyoming were invalid. The developing automotive industry was creating a new middle class society. The song of the day was *I'm Looking Over A Four Leaf Clover*. This truly was "... a brave new world" as Aldous Leonard Huxley had hypothesized and the dollar was king.

The Big Depression

Then came the depression in 1929. I knew nothing of the hardships of the depression that the world was facing in the thirties. I was growing up with no idea of the hard times the majority of people had finding work. My father was a barber and went to work every day, and we always had a good home with enough to eat. We lived only a block from the railroad tracks and I remember, many times, hobos knocking on our back door and asking for something to eat. My mother always gave them a sandwich. I remember over hearing my dad and uncles talking about someone *getting the broom* or *being fired*. I wondered why they were given a broom, and how does one get fired without being burnt. I remember how one of my mother's cousins, uncle John, use to give my brother and I a penny every time he came over to our house and how those pennies stopped when he was out of work.

Detroit

I grew up in Detroit's Southwest side. I had two older brothers and two younger sisters. My oldest brother, Robert, was born in 1924. He was 'a blue baby' and died in May of 1926. My other brother, Albert, was born August 25, 1926. My two younger sisters were Geraldine, born in 1929, and Martha, born in 1933. Geraldine died in 1931. I do not remember the death of my sister Geraldine. In those days, people who died were laid out in their home and a wreath of flowers was hung on the door to signify that someone had died. It was customary for a few relatives of the deceased to stay up all night with the body until the day of the funeral. The children would be sent to stay at a relative's home.

This was the beginning of my journey on the road of life that every one of us must travel. Happenings in our early environment influence us later as the dynamics of a changing world is reflected in our ability to learn right from wrong. What I learned in my youth influenced many of my future decisions—decisions that effected my future successes and failures.

Life is filled with making decisions. What happens tomorrow depends on what decisions we make today. I thought if we make good decisions, good things will happen, and if we make bad decisions, bad things will happen. Even though sometimes with good decisions, bad things can happen. Yet, I felt I should strive to learn the wisdom of making only good and wise decisions—easier said than done.

A New Deal

The election of Franklin D. Roosevelt as President in 1934 and his "nothing to fear but fear itself" started to bring us out of the depression. In 1936, Social Security was enacted along with The National Labor Relations Act to help the "poor working man," and became part of FDR's New Deal. The times seemed to promise a better tomorrow for all, including our family, but in November of that year, my father died.

The day was November 4, 1936, when my dad came home from his barbershop in the middle of the day—not feeling well—he took a hot bath and went to bed. The next morning my dad felt worse so my mother called the doctor (those were the days when doctors made house calls.) The doctor treated him for the common cold or flu. But, the next day, my dad grew worse. On the fourth day, my dad's brother, Gus, called his doctor to come and see his brother,

"Ernie." My dad's doctor was also there. After my uncle's doctor had examined my dad, we overheard the two doctors talking loudly behind closed doors. When they came out of the room, the doctor told us that my dad was dying. He had a burst appendix that had poisoned his system. It was too late to operate and the doctor said there was nothing they could do for him.

My dad, realizing his time was short, asked to see his children. My mother called us into the bedroom. I can still remember my dad's last words as we were brought to the side of his bed.

"Martha," he said to my three-year-old sister, "always stay as sweet as you are ..." Then he turned to me.

"George," he said, "you be good!" I guess I was always testing everything and getting into trouble. But, I remember him saying to me "be good," and I remember thinking that I would be good. My dad then told my brother,

"Albert, you're the man of the house now. Take care of your mother."

Turning to my mother, he said, "Anna, sell the barber shop— keep the car and learn to drive."

After my father died, my mother rented two of our four upstairs bedrooms. First, her brother, uncle Bob and a bachelor cousin rented the rooms paying weekly, and later years "roomers" who worked at the nearby General Motors Ternstedt Plant rented the rooms. I remember my mother putting a "Rooms For Rent" sign in our front window and a picture of "Our Mother of Perpetual Help" next to it. Renting rooms was her only source of income. Somehow she managed to keep the family together and pay her bills. She was very good at budgeting and stretching the dollar to make ends meet. My brother and I got jobs selling magazines and later the Detroit News daily paper to try to help out.

Sometime after my dad died, someone gave us a spitz dog, and we named him Skippy. He was a happy dog and a friend of the whole neighborhood. Every day I would come home from school, I would whistle and call "Skippy!" He would come running out of nowhere to welcome me home. One day, when I called him, I saw him running from across the street right in front of a passing car. He was hit and the man stopped. He was a very nice man and said that he was sorry the dog ran in the street. It was right in front of our house on Military and my mother heard the screeching car as he tried to avoid hitting the dog and came running out to see what was the matter. The man asked me, "Is this your dog?"

"Yes," I said wiping my eyes, "his name's Skippy."

"I'm very sorry," he said. Then turning to my mother, he said, "are you this boys mother?"

"Yes."

"Would you like me to dispose of the dead dog?"

"Yes," she said, "if you will be so kind."

The man picked up the limp body of Skippy and gently put him in the trunk of his car and drove away.

These things I remember about my first real encounter with the death. These images, in later years, would come back to me in vivid memory.

III

SCHOOL DAYS

> *Youth is the opportunity to do something and to become somebody.*
>
> *T. T. Munger—1830-1910 (American Clergyman)*

Three things happened in my youth that would benefit me in later years, as you will see. First, I spent two years in the second grade; second, I learned to tumble as a cheerleader in my sophomore and senior year of high school; and third, I accepted a chance to learn radio repair in my last two years of high school in a program the Catholic schools had with the Detroit Public schools.

I have concluded that what happens in one's life depends more on the individual's decisions rather than on what God directs. What happens tomorrow depends on what we do today. God gives us brains; He expects us to use them. He's not about to perform a miracle to save us if we are going to be stupid about it. God will help us on the way but we must make our own decisions and one decision is to ask for His help.

St. Thomas Aquinas said, "Pray as if everything depends on God, and work as if everything depends on you." But, God works in his own ways that we may find difficult to understand. Maybe God has special plans for all of us that we do not understand. And perhaps the happenings in my youth were designed to prepare me for a special job that God had planned for me in later years.

I also believe that if you love life and wish to see good days, then as the Bible says (Peter 3 verse 10), *For he that would love life and see good days, let him refrain his tongue from evil, and his lips that they speak no guile. Let him eschew evil, and do well—let him seek peace and ensue it.*

As I have said, I like to think that God rules my life and I have nothing to fear. From day one, my parents taught me to have faith in God. My mother had great faith and passed that on to her children. It has helped me travel through this journey in life and still keep my head when all about me are losing theirs. Life is a learning experience with all of its events. And we never stop learning through out our life.

Someone said, "You are what you eat." I think that we could add, you are what your early environment and training prepares and conditions you to be. I think we are a direct product of our early environment and experiences that influence our decisions in life. I felt it was important I make my decisions wisely if I wanted to amount to anything.

When I started school in 1933, I had a problem that I didn't know about. In the second grade, I was having trouble keeping up with reading and writing in English. Because my French parents wanted their children to be fluent in their native tongue, only French was spoken in our home. I was late in learning English. I could speak fluently in French but in the second grade, I was made fully aware of what I was lacking English when I was held back a year. I was expected to keep up with the other children who were five years ahead of me in use of the English language. It didn't bother me and I was not unhappy with this event. However, it would later prove to be very beneficial to me. I remember someone saying, "Learn to read and read books, and you'll never be lonely." I found out that there are books written on everything. Each book has at least one gem in them. Look for that piece of knowledge or gem and go on from there. As a teacher once advised when I was writing my thesis, "first find out what has been written on the subject, then take it one step further." Good advice.

After my dad died in 1936, my brother and I had part time jobs trying to help my mother. I sold the Liberty magazine, The Saturday Evening Post, The Ladies Home Journal and Physical Culture magazines. The magazine manager would deliver them to my home and I would find customers and pay him at the next delivery. The Liberty and Saturday Evening Post were five cents and the Ladies Home Journal was ten cents and the Physical Culture was a quarter. A barbershop was my only customer for the Physical Culture magazine. At the age of twelve, we got newspaper delivery routes for the Detroit News.

At age fifteen, I worked part time for a men's store, washing windows and helping in sales when they were busy. In my junior year, I got a job as an usher at the local Hollywood Theater. Because of my working after school, I was not able to tryout for any sports to earn a school letter. However, regimented practice was not so demanding for the cheerleaders, so, in my Junior year, I joined the Cheer Leading Squad to earn my school letter and became one of five cheer leaders—four Senior boys and one Junior—me.

The next year, my senior year, it was up to me to organize a cheer leading squad. I engaged my close friends, Don Schneider, Jack Brabenac, Melvin Kurpinski in my senior class and Tom Regan, our one junior.

There were five senior girls that wanted to be cheerleaders. And as captain of the Cheerleading squad, I talked to Mother Superior of the IHM nuns for her permission to let these five girls join our cheerleading squad. It would be the only chance for a high school girl to earn a school letter. This was a *first* in the parochial schools and the first time in Redeemer history. We had five girls and five boys. I found a book on tumbling at the local library and the boys all learned how to tumble for our new cheers.

In this last year of high school, our basketball team won a championship and our football team almost won the West Side championship losing only to Lourdes high school.

The 1946 Redeemer Cheer leaders shown above are left to right, bottom row: Mary Barigian, Phyllis Hendrie, Betty McAuliffe, Teresa Rosalik and Joan Diroff. The boys, top row, from left to right are Jack Brabenac, George Arsenault, Melvin Kurpinski, Don Schneider and Tommy Regan.

IV

THE US ARMY

The best armor is to keep out of gunshot.

Francis Bacon 1561-1626

On September 30, 1945, the Second World War was still raging in the Pacific. I was eighteen (draft age), and just starting my senior year in high school. Luckily, the draft board gave this their consideration and I was able to get a deferment from the draft to finish my senior year. Had I not been held back in the second grade, I might have been drafted in June of 1945 and probably shipped out to the Pacific, prior to the war's end in August of 1945. I may have also missed my junior and senior years as a tumbling cheerleader as well as my two years studying radio repair at the Southfield Technical Training Center.

When I graduated from high school in June of 1946, I, with four of my friends, enlisted in the regular army. We knew we had to serve anyway. The Army advertisements were encouraging enlistments promising the "GI Bill." Every day on the radio we would hear that the army had forty thousand jobs that an enlistee could choose from in the regular Army. Also, they were accepting short-term enlistments of eighteen months. The draftees were still being inducted for the duration plus six months—whatever that meant. As an enlistee, I knew the exact date of my discharge—no duration to worry about. The radios kept saying, "Make it a million enlistees for the Army of Occupation and let the boys come home." I started my enlistment on October 1, 1946. My discharge date would be April 1, 1948.

The president of my senior class, Dick Telnack, wanted to enlist in the Navy but they were only taking four-year enlistments. They told him that the Marines across the hall were accepting enlistments for two years. So he became a Marine for two years. When he was discharged, he joined the Trappist Monks in Conyers, Georgia. He helped build a new monastery called The Monastery of the Holy Spirit. As an artist, he designed and built the stained glass windows of their church. He went on to design and build stain glass for churches all over the world. This became his contribution to the Trappist monks and to this day, he has continued his work at the monastery in Georgia.

Fort Sheraton, Chicago, Illinois

The army sent me and other new recruits and enlistees, to Fort Sheraton Chicago where we were given our uniforms and other clothing. We picked up a GI duffle bag, packed with all our issued fatigues, class A uniforms, shirts tie, hat, raincoat, socks, shorts and T shirts. We lugged this now heavy bag to the medical building where we got in line for some kind of shot. The guys coming out told us that they used square needles and some said that they had propellers on the end of the needles. This is where we received our first tetanus shot. With aching arms, we lugged our heavy duffle bag back to a barracks where we changed to our new uniforms. I had forty-four sized under shirts and I took about a thirty-six. Our pants were too long, but I guess that's why we were told to blouse them in our boots.

The next day, we were busy taking IQ tests and getting more shots. The following day, we were given our assignments for training. I was assigned to go to the anti-aircraft replacement-training center at Fort Bliss, Texas. About fifty of us were put on a train heading for Texas. We were seven days on that train because of bad weather, we were told. The diner car ran out of food on the third day, and we were given K rations. There were three kinds of rations. Breakfast, lunch, and dinner. We never knew which one we would be handed. We would trade if we didn't like what we received. The nice part about the K rations, is that they also included candy and cigarettes. Since I was not a smoker at that time, I trade the cigarettes for extra candy.

Fort Bliss, El Paso, Texas

When we arrived at the El Paso train station, it was about three o'clock in the morning. The temperature was about forty-five degrees and we were in our summer uniforms. It was cold standing on the station platform. Finally some trucks pulled up. A Sergeant jumped out of the truck and yelled, "Alright, lets get these men out of this hot sun." I'll never forget that because that was opposite what I was thinking.

At camp, we went into the mess hall and they served us hot coffee. I didn't drink coffee, so all I had was a glass of water. That was my introduction to Fort Bliss. I found myself assigned to Battery B of the 58th Anti Aircraft Battalion. We were being trained to fire, disassemble and reassemble the M1 rifle and an automatic sub machine gun, called the grease gun. This weapon was made with a stiff wire attached to what appeared to be a piece of pipe. We learned to shoot the grease gun in bursts of three because the gun would tend to climb upward and to the right as you fired it. The grease gun uses 45-caliber ammunition making it very lethal at close range.

Basic training was hectic for me, to say the least. I wondered if I'd ever get out of it. Would it ever be over? Every hour of every day, the army had us busy marching, running the obstacle course, attending lectures and doing calisthenics. There was many a night that I was assigned to do Guard Duty and many a day I was assigned to KP (kitchen police) duty. I found out that the battery clerk assigned guard duty and KP alphabetically. So, Arsenault was one of the first for both. (Incidentally, in the Army, they only used your last name. We got use to calling everyone by his last name.) When I was assigned KP and Guard Duty for the second time while some guys had not yet been assigned, I asked the our training Cadre, "why?" He said the battery clerk got mixed up on his list so he started the alphabet over. I'll bet there's a guy named Tom Zink somewhere who never had KP or Guard duty.

I found out that, in the army, the word *police* meant to pick up and clean up. When we were told to police the area, they didn't mean *guard duty,* they meant to clean up the area. We were told that if we saw something on the ground, pick it up. If we can't pick it up, paint it. And if it moved, salute it. I learned that every morning, you better check the bulletin board outside the mess hall for your name. It was here that we were told who was on KP and who was on guard duty, as well as other assignments.

It was during basic training that the army gave us more immunization shots for various diseases. There were many days when we were told to change to strip down to only raincoats and boots and they would march us to the medical buildings where we would stand in long lines waiting to enter a building. We were never told what was up. Many times they would give us a shot in the arm and on another occasion of raincoats and boots standing in line, was for a dental check up. It is during basic training that any dental work you might need was done. The army didn't bother asking you if you would like to have dental work, they told you. That's an order! Now I knew what was meant in the saying, "you never know where you're going until you get there." And, "hurry up and wait."

I had some cavities that needed attention. It seemed that every Monday, I was on the roster for the dentist. I would have rather have gone with my buddies, but in the Army they don't ask you what you want, they tell you. One thing I can say about the dental work the Army did for me was that I never had a tooth ache again.

The basic training was too regimented for my taste. Our days were detailed from morning to night. We did have Saturdays and Sundays off. There was a recreation room with pool tables, ping-pong and games. The Autumn weather on the desert is hot every day and cold every night. To make matters worse, the wind, at night, would blow sand through the hut-vents. In the mornings we had sand all over the inside of our huts. We had to shake the sand out of our blankets and sweep the hut floors each day. Nighttime was my time! I was happy every night to be left alone in my bed, in our four man huts.

I remember one night a wild thunderstorm hit our huts in this desert. The wind howled and the thunder rattled with lightning and the rain came down all over our battery streets beating on the roofs of our huts. The heavens pounded down on this man's army in a ferocious violent manner. I remember thinking that God was still the Almighty and He was still in charge. He had the final control of the world in spite of the U. S. Army. I love storms to this day. The more lightning and noisier the storms are the better.

U. S. Army Signal Corps

My basic training came to an end the third week of November. We were again waiting for our new assignments. I had studied Radio Repair as a subject in high school. I spoke to the company commander asking for a possible transfer to the Signal Corps. Much to my surprise, I received special orders by the command of Colonel King to transfer to Fort Dix, New Jersey for further training in the Signal Corps. All my buddies in the 58th Battalion were on orders to go to Korea as had been rumored. I had avoided Korea for the time being.

I met three other GIs on the train from Fort Bliss who were also on orders to transfer to Fort Dix, New Jersey. The train from Texas was scheduled to arrive in Chicago the day before Thanksgiving where we would transfer to a train for New Jersey. However, when we reached Chicago, we decided that we would go home for Thanksgiving. One of us, Private James H. Scott, said he had a car and he volunteered to pick us up at our homes and we would all drive to New Jersey on Friday. The train we were to transfer to would not arrive in New Jersey until Friday anyway.

I took a cab to the airport and luckily, there was a plane getting ready to leave for Detroit. I bought my ticket and the clerk said, "I'll tell the pilot to wait for you but you'd better hurry." I was in uniform and it was amazing that everyone was happy to help a GI. I started for the plane, suitcase and duffle bag over my shoulder, when a redcap ran up to me and asked if he could help. "Yes!" I said, handing him my heavy duffle bag. Together we ran out of the building and on to the tarmac towards a plane waiting with the engines already running. They had the door of the plane open and a stairway up to the plane. As I ran, I reached into my pocket and grabbing a dollar, I handed it to the redcap as he gave me the duffle bag. I climbed the stairs where the airline stewardess showed me a seat in first class. "You're lucky soldier," she said. We don't often hold up a plane flight for just anybody and then let him sit in first class. Your lucky you're a GI." I knew I was lucky—I was in uniform.

My mother was surprised to see me home. It was a great Thanksgiving. All my relatives came over to see me. I had a great home cooked meal. I was happy to see my mother, sister and brother and sleep in my own bed again. Some of my friends and neighbors came over to see me and wish me luck in the army. It gave me a good feeling to see all of them. I was proud to be in uniform.

Friday afternoon, James Scott, my army buddy, with his car arrived as planned. We drove to Toledo and it was getting dark when a police car stopped us just before the Pennsylvania turnpike. Now what? I thought. Are we going to get arrested for going home for Thanksgiving? The officer's searched our car and we showed them our orders to transfer to Fort Dix, New Jersey. They said, "Ok soldiers, you can go. But get that back license plate light fixed." I'll bet there was more to it then a burned out license plate light. I suppose they were wondering where these soldiers were going at this time of night.

Fort Dix, New Jersey

It was early in the morning when we arrived at Fort Dix. The MP at the gate directed us to a barracks where a sergeant took our papers and assigned us a bunk. It was Thanksgiving weekend and the sergeant was a little tipsy. He kept talking about the Second World War in Europe and how he had walked across Germany as a combat engineer: "I carried my coffin and a shovel all across France and Germany," he said. "I buried many of my buddies and I was ready for the same."

On Monday, I found myself in a new basic training company. I was starting basic training all over again. A week went by. Payday came, but I was not paid. I went to see the First Sergeant. He sent me to the Adjutant General—an officer who, I was told, was the serviceman's lawyer. I gave him my copy of my orders that I had received when I left Fort Bliss, Texas. He said that I would not have to take basic training again and he told me that the army would be sending all available men who had finished their basic training to Korea. "However, in your case," he said, "We are unable to find your papers. Until we find your papers, we can not do anything." Meanwhile, he put me on their casual list and excused me from taking basic training again. He gave me an advance on my pay and a pass if I wanted to go home for the Christmas holidays. I decided to hitch hike home over the Pennsylvania Turnpike and fly back after Christmas. I had no trouble getting rides.

For the next few weeks, I spent my time in the library and the PX. I wrote my mother that I would probably be sent to Korea. She wrote back that she was praying that I would not be sent overseas. Needless to say, I had missed another payday at the end of December, but this time—I didn't say a word. The second week in January, just as the adjutant general had told me, a notice went up on the bulletin board stating that all casual personnel would be put on orders to be transferred to Korea. Strange as it may seem, when the shipment of men went out, my name was not on that list. I surmised that my records had not yet been found. Once again I had avoided Korea. I preferred stateside duty if I could get it.

Fort Monmouth, New Jersey

Nine days after the New Year, my records were found and I was given orders for further training in the Signal Corps at Fort Monmouth, New Jersey. When I arrived at Fort Monmouth, I was told that although I had previous schooling in radio repair, unless I extended my enlistment to three years I did not qualify for radio repair school. I told them I didn't want to extend my enlistment to three years. My plans were to go to college with the GI bill after my eighteen-month enlistment. They said they would schedule me to study to be a Central Office Technician. This was a six-month duration. My job would be the installation and servicing of PBX telephone equipment.

I learned that I was the only short-term enlistee in the school. Everyone I spoke to was a long-term enlistee. I therefore made it my business to study hard. I was afraid that they would not let me finish. Six months later I finished at the top of my class. I received the United States Army Signal School Certificate as a Central Office Technician classification of 095.

I loved the school and even though we still had KP and Guard Duty, I was happy with this arrangement. I loved marching to school every morning in full "class A" uniform with a marching military band leading us. I received my graduation Certificate July 28, 1947.

Fort Monmouth, New Jersey

The Signal School

Be it known that

PFC HENRY ARSENAULT

having been found qualified in the

CENTRAL OFFICE TECHNICIAN COURSE

at The Signal School
United States Army, is hereby awarded this

Certificate

In testimony whereof and by virtue of
authority vested in us by the War Department
we hereby affix our signatures and
the seal of this institution,

at Fort Monmouth, New Jersey, this ___28th___ day of ___July___ 19 47

ASSISTANT COMMANDANT

Lt. Col., Sig. C. SECRETARY

Col, Sig C COMMANDANT

U.S. Army Signal Corps Central Office Technician Certificate

V

ARMY LIFE

All the world's a stage

And one man is his time plays many parts.

William Shakespeare 1564-1616

"So you're Henry Arsenault!" the desk sergeant said, as I was being interviewed for final assignment after completing my school requirements. He looked up at me from his desk. "Your name kept coming up every month for the last six months. How did a 'short-timer' like you get into this school? If it wasn't for your straight 'A' grades, I would have had you out of here a long time ago."

He sent me for an interview to the Signal Corps Engineering Laboratory Development Detachment on the Fort for possible job openings in the Signal Corps' Engineering Laboratories.

At SCELDD, a 1st lieutenant interviewed me. "I see by your records, you studied radio repair. What do you know the best?" he asked, "radio repair that you studied in high school, or central office that you just finished studying here?"

"Radio repair", I said, "I studied radio repair for two years in high school and I have a letter of recommendation signed by my school instructor listing all my studies."

"Hmm," he said reading the letter I handed him. Then looking down at the paper on his desk, he said, "We have an opening for a radio repairman in our Signal Corps Engineering Development Detachment at "Coles Engineering Laboratory," he then looked me straight in the eye and said, "Do you think you can handle it?"

"Of course, that's the kind of work I was trying to get back at Fort Bliss, Texas."

"OK, it's your job!" he stood up and shook my hand. "Good luck, soldier."

United States Signal Corps Engineering Development Detachment

I couldn't have planned it better. Life was great. It was a great job. I had the opportunity to work with civilian scientists as well as with German engineers who spoke with a heavy accent. They couldn't have been more polite and considerate. I was the only uniformed person in the Coles Short Range Radio laboratory section. I did miscellaneous tasks for them as needed, such as getting parts and hardware from the crib and testing short-range hardware and equipment for specific specifications.

H. George Arsenault in Army Uniform

I was promoted to a 'T5'. We use to say, "a T5 is a Corporal,—technician with brains." I received a permanent pass to leave the Fort. I had no KP or guard duty. I had a five-days-a-week job from 8am to 5pm, with weekends off with a permanent pass to leave the camp. What a life after basic training!

U.S. Army Signal Corps Engineering Development Detachment
(I'm 3ʳᵈ from the left in the 2ⁿᵈ row.)

Every month-end, after payday, we went to Manhattan where servicemen had free tickets to Broadway and radio shows and free lunches at the Soldiers and Sailors Club. We called it "the invasion of Manhattan Island." The fort had a good library, theatre and PX on the grounds with cut-rate costs that we could all afford. The PX served 3.2 beers to all soldiers for a small price. There were dances every Saturday at the PX attended by girls from and around the

Fort. I didn't know how to dance and I was too shy to try, so I would just watch.

The GI Theatre Group

There was a theatrical group of GIs who were preparing to put on the play "Winterset." The Company Bulletin Board had a notice up asking for those who wanted to try out for this play. I tried out and was given the part of "Pedro, the organ grinder." I had a speaking part of two lines—"Whatsa da matter? You no lika the music?" It was a good play off Broadway in the thirties about gangsters in New York City. One poignant line I'll never forget is when the hero of the play states a chess move then asks a question. As I remember, he says, "White to play and mate in three moves. Why does white always win and black always lose? Suppose black were to win and white were to lose, what then? Well, then, black would be white and white would be black; as it often is; as we often are. Right makes white; losers turn black."

Every one in the play received a Commendation from the Regiment Commander to go into our records. The theater group asked me to take the part of Groucho Marks in a play called "The Man Who Came to Dinner" but I would be leaving the Army before the play was scheduled to run so I had to turn it down.

In those days, everyone was proud to be in uniform. People gave us first class treatment wherever we went. At theaters, they always let us go to the head of the line. Everyone was friendly and spoke to us like they all knew us, as if we were relatives. I was getting the benefits and respect that was really earned by all the men and women who had gone overseas and put their life on the line for the past four years for love of their country.

Manhattan's Broadway, Fifth Avenue, Time Square, was a land of magic that would be alive with people till all hours of the morning. It was similar to what Disneyland, Atlantic City, or Las Vegas is today. We visited the observation tower of the Empire State Building and we even went to Coney Island amusement park. Those month-end weekends in Manhattan were great. It was there where I tasted my first pizza pie, except in 1947 they called it "tomato pie."

Coles Laboratories

Another example I could cite to support the power of my mother's and my aunt's prayers that seemed to follow me, was during my assignment to Signal Corps' Coles Laboratories in New Jersey. One day, I was sent to help a captain and a sergeant move some crates of heavy radio equipment. A truckload of crates was to be moved to a warehouse for storage. "Climb on top of the boxes, Arsenault, and you can ride to the warehouse with us," the sergeant said.

The sergeant and the Captain were riding in the truck cab and I was sitting on top of the boxes on the bed of this stake truck when I felt the boxes I was sitting on move as the truck was rounding a curve. The next thing I knew, I was flying through the air with boxes falling all around me. I remember that it was the same feeling that I had experience in high school when doing flips in my cheerleading days. I had become quite good at tumbling. My trained reaction when being thrown from the truck was to tumble in a relaxed manner as soon as I touched ground. The truck screeched to a stop and the captain and the sergeant came running up to me as I lay on the ground.

"Don't move, soldier!" The sergeant shouted.

Why not? I thought, trying to feel my side where I rolled as I hit the ground.

At that moment the captain arrived at my side. Putting his hand on my shoulder, he said, "Don't try to move, not yet. How do you feel? Any pain anywhere?" He asked.

"No! I'm OK."

"Can you move your fingers?"

"Sure."

"Good, your neck's not broken. How about your toes?"

"Yes, I can move them too", I said, doing so.

"Good! Your back is not broken. Now wait, don't move not yet," the sergeant said as he lit up a cigarette and handed it to me.

I took a few puffs. "Can I get up now?"

"OK, but move very slowly and tell me if you feel any pain."

So I moved slowly and I could feel a sting along my upper right leg. "I'm okay", I said, "just some scratches on the side of my leg where my pants are torn."

"Soldier, there must be somebody praying for you," the captain said. "I thought we'd be picking up a bag of bones. You're lucky those boxes didn't fall on top of you. You sure you're okay?"

"Sure, I'm okay," I said as I stood.

"I want you to report to medical right away. Tell them what happened," he said. "It's in building A on the other side of those buildings across the field. Do you think you can walk that far?"

"Sure!"

"After you get out of there, take a shuttle back to the Fort and take the rest of the day off," the Captain said. "Tell them I said so. Let me know if there's any trouble."

"Yes sir," I said saluting him.

Letters

I reported to the medical first aid and the nurse put some medication on the scratches and bruises on my leg and sent me to the gate to catch a shuttle back to my barracks.

When I arrived there, I found a letter from my mother. "Are you all right?" she wrote, "Last night I had a dream that you fell off a truck. I could see you very clearly. You had a fresh haircut. I've been praying for you ever since."

Coincidence … who knows? I always thought my mother was a saint and had connections with God.

When I finished my eighteen months in the Army, I received the finest letter of recommendation I could have hoped for from R.

A. Morris, Chief of Short-Range Equipment Section of the U. S. Army Signal Corps Engineering Laboratories. I thought I had been given a reputation that I will certainly try to live up to and hope to deserve.

They had even offered me a job as a civilian working in Coles Laboratories and after reading the letter, I wondered if I had made a mistake leaving New Jersey and this job offer.

HEADQUARTERS
SIGNAL CORPS ENGINEERING LABORATORIES
FORT MONMOUTH, NEW JERSEY

REFER TO: ADDRESS REPLY TO:

22 March 1948

To Whom it May Concern:

        This is to certify that the undersigned has known T-5
Henry Arsenault for 8 months.

        Mr. Arsenault has a wealth of experience along radio
technical lines and has served under me in the capacity of
Technician 5th Grade, Radio Repairman for the past 8 months.
The undersigned regards the abilities of Mr. Arsenault very
highly and expresses the utmost confidence in him.

        In my business dealings with Mr. Arsenault, I have
found him to be sincere, reliable, conscientious, and tireless
in his efforts to render service. He appears to be able to
analyze any situation calmly and quickly under adverse conditions.

        He is courteous, trustworthy, interested in his work,
and loyal to his supervisors. He is cooperative in his work
with others, is well liked, and respected by all his associates.

        The services of Mr. Arsenault have been exceptionally
satisfactory and the undersigned regrets that he will no longer
be a part of this Office.

                                   Very truly yours,

                                   R. A. MORRIS
                                   Chief, Short Range Equipment Section
                                   Radio Communication Branch

U.S. Army SCELDD Letter of Recommendation

The Dark Ages

These war years … remind me of what a college history professor once said: "We are living in the dark ages of mankind. A few thousand years from now, this era may well be looked on as barbaric and uncivilized. We are primitive savages, just barely out of the bush, mostly barbaric."

I believe that he was very close to the truth. If we consider the millions that died in World War II including the systematic execution of many millions in Nazi death camps, we can get some idea of what this historian was talking about. We have just begun our human existence and we have yet to become civilized. The human race has barely scratched the surface of enlightenment and man's humanity.

That's why I believe Christ came at the very earliest possible moment in time. He came at the very birth of a civilization that could grasp Divine understanding. Christ planted the beginning seeds of the dignity of man that could mature to a total humanized world in some future century.

Honorable Discharge

On March 31, 1948, my eighteen-month enlistment was up and I received an Honorable discharge from the Regular Army with the GI Bill locked in. Now I could go to college for eighteen months with all tuition, expenses plus 75 dollars monthly-authorized subsistence.

I was proud to have been a part of the Signal Corps Engineering Laboratories. President, Harry Truman, sent me a letter thanking me for serving my country. I'm sure all GIs who were discharged at that time received a letter from old HST, but I felt good getting my letter.

HENRY G. ARSENAULT

To you who answered the call of your country and served in its Armed Forces to bring about the total defeat of the enemy, I extend the heartfelt thanks of a grateful Nation. As one of the Nation's finest, you undertook the most severe task one can be called upon to perform. Because you demonstrated the fortitude, resourcefulness and calm judgment necessary to carry out that task, we now look to you for leadership and example in further exalting our country in peace.

Harry Truman

THE WHITE HOUSE

Harry S. Truman Congratulatory for Service Letter

It took a year, after the fighting ceased, for Congress to officially declare the war over and the Victory Medal was issued to all personnel that were in the armed forces at the end of 1946, so I received mine just after my basic training. That's the only medal I received. That medal and my SCEL-DD letter of recommendation plus my letter from Harry Truman are my only trophies from my army days.

These army days taught me how to live harmoniously with many in one building. It also taught me that some hard work studying and with someone else's prayers could be a contributing factor for my successful enlistment tour in the United State's Regular Army.

VI

THE GI BILL

> *In the world's broad field of battle;*
>
> *In the bivouac of life;*
>
> *Be not like dumb driven cattle.*
>
> *Be a hero in the strife!*
>
> *Henry Wadsworth Longfellow (1807-1882)*

The first twenty or twenty-five years of anyone's life are filled with education and training, both formal and informal. It's as if when you are born, you should be told, "Welcome to the human race. Now, here's what you will have to do and not do and here's what you have to know …" It's a catch-up game for the first twenty five years. After that, you spend the next twenty-five or thirty years trying to make the first twenty-five years of study and learning pay off.

From the beginning to the end of life, events such as world economic depressions, wars, marriage, children and death often change the direction of our lives and enrich or degrade us. Sometimes, these events destroy what we deem good in our lives. How can we explain this? How can we defend ourselves against a sea of trouble?

In 1950, President Harry S. Truman used his wartime powers to declare a 'police action' in Korea. This may have been a first on a world scale; Americans were now fighting in an undeclared war overseas. Many of my former high school classmates who had avoided the draft since graduation were now being called into service and sent to Korea. I knew that Korea was a hot spot back in 1946 when I first entered the army. All the officers were predicting that Korea would be our next war.

Luckily, I had already served my country and was out of the army by the time the Korean War started. My mother was still praying for me, I now surmise, and I once more was "delivered from evil." I consider war as evil. I didn't do a lot of praying in those days and that's why today I say, "someone was praying for me." And I'm sure that my mother and her two sisters in the convent were praying for me as they often told me.

I have come to believe that much of what happens tomorrow depends on what we do today. We are not designed by God to be contented cows, chewing on our cud. We all need to be challenged. We need challenges to experience the joy of success and the feeling of accomplishment. That's when fun comes into our lives.

With my honorable discharge on April 1, 1948, the GI Bill gave me a month of college tuition with expenses for every month of my enlistment plus 75 dollars a month subsistence. I first applied at the University of Detroit to enter its Engineering Department. Since I was pretty good at radio and telephone repair, I felt I should study and become an electrical engineer.

But, I did not have enough high school math and science. While I had studied radio repair for two years in high school, I had missed out on geometry, trigonometry, biology and chemistry. Since I would have to spend a year making up those subjects, I would only have six months of paid tuition from the GI Bill left to complete a four to five year endeavor. At that time, student loans, grants and scholarships were not prevalent.

Detroit College of Business

Following the path of least resistance, I decided on a Business School where I would earn an associates degree in two years without any make-up courses. This would be only three months short of what the GI Bill would pay. I would have to pay the last three months (a semester) myself. I had studied typing and business in high school. So, as in nature, I took the path of least resistance and registered at Detroit College of Business. And that's how I became an accountant.

Since all returning veterans were guaranteed their old jobs back, I returned to The Detroit News where I had been a part time copy boy for a year before I had enlisted and I was given an evening desk job in Display Advertising thus allowing me to go to college full-time during the day.

However, immature as I was, I kept that job for only two months. I wanted to spend all my time in school without work interfering with my studies. I know now that I would have been better off staying at the News where they were being so nice to me. It's another example of positive thinking: if you think you can—you can. And, if you think you can't, then you can't. If you begin with a negative attitude, you're two strikes down right from the start.

I now know that I could have worked, gone to school, and done even better, grade-wise, if I had thought I could and wanted it. At the Signal Corps School in the army, I had done just that. Also, six years later, I returned to Business College and did just that. I completed the last semester I had missed when the GI Bill had run out and I didn't have the money to finish at that time. This time I had decided I could, even though I was married with a family and I did.

I not only acquired the Associate's Degree, but I managed to get my Bachelor's Degree from the Detroit College of Business and my Master's Degree from the University of Detroit, thanks to the General Motors Employee Educational Reimbursement Program.

So, I say, you have to believe that you can and you may surprise yourself as to what you really can do.

Education

I have often thought about our system of education. I feel and believe that every citizen in this great country should have the opportunity for as much education as they would aspire to have. The whole world should have free education for all who would pursue learning, without consideration as to race, color or creed. All world citizens, like the early Romans, should have the right to education at any school in the world any time in their life, with no tuition.

I believe as stated in the Declaration of Independence, that all men are "... endowed by their creator with certain inalienable rights; that among these are life, liberty, and the pursuit of happiness ..." and I believe that "the pursuit of happiness" requires "education." I believe that this is a truth also "... to be self evident."

It is easy to observe that an educated person has the advantage over those who are less educated. It is obvious that life becomes better for that person and his or her world. Therefore, no one should be kept out of any university because of lack of money. The best thing that my service in the Army did for me was to give me the GI Bill. This Bill educated millions of Americans and gave us the chance to seek higher education. If you have the will and desire, your education should be free and unlimited.

Free college education should be the goal in this nation, the same as elementary education is today. Education should be a process that never ends. Trial and error is a method of self-education, but it is wasteful and time consuming. It is much easier to seek teachers who have spent their lives studying the subject and learn from them where the state of the art is today and start from there to make your contribution to this world.

The first few years into the fifties after I had left the army, I was completely concerned and absorbed with trying to get an education. There were certain habits I had to discontinue and certain new habits I had to pursue, such as reading and studying. The computer axiom, *garbage in, garbage out* is highly applicable here. Don't just read books—be selective. Read only good books, not garbage. It's bad enough that our environment fills our world with pollution and trash: the least we can do is to be selective when we have the option, and not fill our brains with pollution and trash. Don't just turn television on to see what's on; find out first from the schedule and then select what may be worthwhile, something that will make you a better person, not worse.

Christ said, "Seek and you shall find." I think that we should seek education and we will find it. Christ seems to be saying, "Don't give up." Psychiatrists tell us that we only use a very small part of our God-given brain. Every one of us has the capacity to do more and do better, if we try. Somebody said, "To try and fail is at least to learn; to fail to try is to suffer the immeasurable loss of what might have been."

During these early years of trying to obtain a formal education, I wrote a poem called *Relentless* to perk up my spirits.

RELENTLESS

The thought of the future;
Still inspires
Of castle and kingdoms,
And great empires.

A wondrous feeling;
For great achievement;
Though it be only
For self-appeasement.

Where others have failed,
I will succeed.
Like a relentless tale;
I will proceed.

And though black seem the sky;
And failures in sight;
I'll never say 'die!'
I'll keep up the fight.

And when victory's at hand,
I'll say with a grin,
Shake hands with a man,
That knows how to win.

It was with these thoughts that I entered the fifties, full of hope and promise for the future. I had a good job as bookkeeper for Frank L. Mayhew, Wholesale Beef and Veal. I bought a new car and it seemed that nothing could go wrong. All I had to do was 'hang in there and fight'. I could hear in my mind's ear the words of, *Stout Hearted Men, I'll Buy That Dream* and *My Blue Heaven.*

VII

THE RUN AROUND

Every man's life is a fairy tale, written by God's fingers

Hans Christian Anderson

The year was 1951 when I met a girl named Margaret Elizabeth Foley. She lived only a few blocks from my house on Military street and we both had attended Holy Redeemer Catholic School. Although she was two years younger and an under-classman during my high school years, I had never met her. It wasn't until she was 21 and I was 23, that a mutual friend, Bernadette Mulligan, introduced her to me. Bernadette Mulligan was a member of a glee club of former classmates that I had joined after I was back from the US Army.

Bernadette was about five years older then I, and though we were friends, I noticed that when we went out together without the glee club, we would never go anywhere that her other friends might be. I guess she felt she was 'robbing the cradle' as the saying went in those days. One day, Bernadette said to me, "George, I've got the perfect girl for you, and I want you to meet her!"

Now, that's funny, I thought, why is she looking for the perfect girl for me? It must be the matchmaker instinct in older women.

"Is that right?" I answered. "I hope she's pretty."

"She's beautiful and she lives just four blocks from you."

54

"I'm game. When is this going to happen?"
"I'll ask her over tomorrow night and you be there to meet her."
"That's fine with me."

And that's how I met Marge. She was great from the beginning. She was as pretty as a picture and just as sweet as she was pretty. She was unpretentious, kind, easygoing, considerate and empathetic and wise. Everybody loved her. I couldn't help falling for her. She was so nice.

I grew up with the old song *I want a girl just like the girl that married dear old dad* ringing in my ears. And here she was. I had visions of someday marrying this perfect girl. I liked to picture myself as a perfect gentleman, a knight in shining armor on a white horse winning the heart of his fair lady with brave deeds. I use to tell everyone that my mother raised me to be a gentleman. The romance of my life would have to be a real lady, like my mother.

The age of chivalry is still here as far as I was concerned. I wanted (like in the song) *a Sunday kind of love … the kind to last past Saturday night … a little more than love at first sight.* She was my perfect girl. I treated her like a princess and she treated me like a prince. Who could ask for anything more?

After a few weeks, it seemed that I was seeing her every day. We just felt comfortable together and before long I was teasing her about marriage. "We might as well get married," I would say, "and stop all this foolishness of me coming over here every day. I could save on gas, and your parents insisting that you get home every night at a 'decent hour' is ridiculous. Your twenty one years old!"

"Not me!" she would answer. "I'm not the marrying kind!"

That was her standard answer, yet I continued with my standard question: "When are you going to say yes and marry me?"

One evening while we were out with another couple, the conversation turned to marriage and children. "Well," I said, "if I ever have any boys, they're going to learn the value of money early. I will expect them to have a paper route like I had and their own savings bank account to teach them the habit of saving, like my mother did for me."

"I think that if I ever have any girls," Marge said, "they will learn how to keep house and cook while they're still young and not like what happened at my mother's house."

"What happened at your house?" I asked.

"At our house there was my grandmother, my mother, my god mother and five children. We were never allowed in the kitchen between meals. We were never taught anything about cooking, cleaning or washing dishes. The three 'ladies' would do all that."

"They must have thought that three women cooking in the kitchen was already too many women," I said.

"I guess so, I'm not sure I could even boil water to this day."

"That's too bad," I said, "but you can read and anybody who can read can learn anything. There are *how-to books* on everything, especially cookbooks. Anyway, I'm on your side, Marge. I think that children should have chores and be expected to help around the house, and they should be included in all family affairs including the decision-making for family affairs. Children do not want to be a burden on their parents. I know I didn't and they do want to help and contribute. I know I did."

"Absolutely!" my friend Bob declared. "Children are part of the fun of being married and it's the family that makes it fun."

"Agreed," I said. "And here's another thing: I believe one should try to plan on having children while you're still young, say in your twenties. That way you're not an old man when they mature and you can still buddy-up with them for more fun ... right?"

"Right!" Bob said, "like going fishing, camping, or to the ball game."

"That's the idea," I said, nodding my head in agreement.

The conversation turned to other things, but little did I realize what had just been discussed was giving Marge some ideas. Later that evening, when I was dropping Marge off at her home, I offered my usual query, "Will you marry me and stop all this 'I have to be home at a decent hour' business?"

She took me by surprise and said, "Maybe I will."

"What did you say?" I stammered.

"Maybe I will," she replied. "Tonight, when we were talking about marriage and children with Bob and Alice, I couldn't help thinking that 'your' children and 'my' children were 'our' children."

I couldn't believe my ears. Marge was actually saying 'maybe' after all these months of my teasing her. I wasn't prepared for that answer. I had anticipated her usual, "I'm not the marrying kind." This was a new answer. Now what do I do—I thought. I'd never gotten this far before.

"What do you mean by 'maybe'?" I asked.

"I have something to tell you," Marge said. "Nine years ago, when I was thirteen, I had a brain tumor operation. I'm all right now, I guess, but before we can even plan on getting married, I want to have a complete physical examination at Ford's Hospital and get the doctor's okay."

"Are you serious? You had a brain tumor operation?"

"Yep!"

"But you're okay now … right?"

"Oh, sure, as far as I know. But I still want to be absolutely certain. So, that's why I said 'maybe' until I can get a doctor's clean bill of health I'm not marrying anyone. I was really sick nine years ago and it wouldn't be right to put you through the worry that my parents had at that time. I had double vision, loss of balance, nausea—-and terrible headaches.

My father and mother were worried sick, and my father, being a good Irish Catholic, got some water from Lourdes in France and blessed me with it every day. He also took me to see a very holy priest who was here at a Capuchin monastery on the eastside of Detroit. His name was Father Casey Solanus. Rumors were that he had performed many miracles and my father wasn't leaving a stone unturned. But I kept getting worse until finally I went into the hospital for more tests and then they operated. They operated right at the back of my head.

After the operation, the doctor told my parents that in about three weeks I could go back to school. Right after the operation, I felt fine. I didn't have those headaches or dizziness and no double vision. They called it a miracle," she said. "My parents had been praying for a miracle and the nuns in school told me that God must have great things planned for me. The nuns wanted me to join the convent and become a Sister of the Immaculate Heart of Mary … an IHM nun, like them, of course."

"Did you want to be a nun?"

"Not really. But when the sisters said I should, it caused me to think about it for a long time."

"Well, Father Solanus didn't say that you should become a nun, did he?"

"No, he just said that I would be all right."

"And he was right. You are all right now…. right?"

"Oh sure. But you can see why I need to be certain before I get married. It wouldn't be fair to you otherwise. That's why I always said, 'I'm not the marrying kind'. I always wondered if maybe I should have joined the IHMs and become a nun."

"Well, as far as I'm concerned, you're fine by me…. and that's what's important. Besides there's more than one-way to get to heaven … and being a good parent is a tougher job and more important than being a nun. Now, I'm not taking anything away from the nuns, but everyone has to look for their own vocation in this world. And I thing your vocation is with me."

Decisions

After leaving Marge, I was so confused that I didn't see her for three straight days. I was befuddled. I didn't know what was right and wrong. I asked my brother, Al, what he thought about my getting married. He looked at me with a puzzled expression on his face and said, "Well, if life gets dull, get married and it won't be dull any more." He was right. Life was never dull after my marriage.

I was unsure what direction would be the correct one for me to take. Maybe, I thought, the nuns were right and she should become a nun. Then, again, maybe I should be a priest. But where would the world be if everyone were to become nuns and priests? It would be the end of the world—no more children. No, I'm right! Everyone must find his own vocation in God's plan. The fact that she had a miracle and was 'saved for great things' as the nuns told her doesn't mean that she should become a nun. I'm happy with her and she's happy with me and that's what most important. I'm sure God didn't want the both of us to be miserable all our lives.

When Christ went to the wedding at Cana, I'm sure that he wasn't crying when he changed the water into wine and the people were rejoicing—celebrating for a good reason. Christ approved and sanctioned weddings, marriages, children, and families. I pondered and prayed for the right answer. To wed or not to wed, that was my question. I decided that she was the kind of a person for me and whatever children God might send us would be okay. I would be proud to say to my children, "this is your mother that I chose for you." And if the Almighty gives me fifty years with her or ten years or whatever, it would be better than no years. So, who cares what the doctors might say, I thought.

She can have her physical, but no matter what the results…. if she will have me as I am, then I will take her as she is. I'll insist that we be married even if the doctors give her a negative report. What do they know, anyway? I read where a doctor said, "half of what we learn in medicine is wrong except we don't know which half." All her problems are in the past anyway. What do I care about the past? It's now and the future that is more important.

No one knows how many years they have left—even doctors. A brain tumor operation when she was thirteen—humbug—I couldn't care less. She apparently miraculously survived and that's it. So be it. Remember, George, I said to myself, still reinforcing my decision, she did finish high school and she was now gainfully employed with General Motors as a teletype operator. You're not sick when you can do that. What do you need, George? I asked myself. It's the writing on the wall. Remember Father Solanus apparently did perform a miracle. She may be a little unsteady in her balance when jumping over a puddle, but she's just as normal as anyone else—and a lot smarter than your average person and twice as nice—and she loves me. Who could ask for anything more? I wrote a poem for Marge. I called it *The Language of the Heart*. I have lost the poem but the last stanza remains with me and explains my feeling about love and marriage. It goes like this:

The Language of the Heart
So, if my voice speaks not the words you seek.
My actions are my words of smart.
For words are not yet made to speak,
The language of the heart.

VIII

STILL LEARNING

> *Life is a long lesson in humility.*
>
> *Sir James M. Barrie 1860-1937*

Bill Reeber was a very good friend of mine. His father owned a furniture store on West Warren and 23rd Street and we were in the Glee Club together where I had met Bernadette Mulligan. It was during this time when I was courting Margaret that my boss at GM Fleetwood plant sent me to a Dale Carnegie evening course at the GM Building on *How to Win Friends And Influence People.* Dale Carnegie had written a book by the same name

Public speaking was the main subject. But, I did learn something about how to win friends and influence people in taking this course that I have never forgotten.

The instructor said, "we can win friends by taking an interest in people. Talk about them and their plans, hopes, desires and their life. Take a sincere and honest interest and let them know it. As your homework, I want everyone to try this on a not-to-close friend or neighbor and make a report in a couple of weeks."

I decided that I would try this on Jim Reeber, Bill's younger brother. I would only see Jim when I would stop at their store. He never came with Bill and I when we would go out. Jim had his own friends: a few years younger then Bill and I. He had a girl friend that he was planning to marry. So, as part of my homework, every day I would see Jim, I would go out of my way to say hello and ask him about his upcoming wedding plans. He would go into detail of all the things that they were planning for before and after the wedding. Much to my amazement, Jim began to go out of his way to say hello to me. After a couple of weeks of this, Jim surprised me by asking me to be in his wedding. I had to accept but I sure was amazed.

Now, I'm not a person who aspired for a large family right from my youth. As I had often said, "a boy for you and a girl for me" seemed to me as the perfect size family for anyone. However, I had the occasion during the time I was courting Marge to be shocked with numbers in the size of a family. It happened one day when I was working repairing dealer radios in the basement of the Reeber Furniture Company.

"George," Bill said, "how would you like to go to a séance with me? I just delivered some furniture to this lady on 23rd Street and she told me that she holds séances. She said she'd give me a special free session. I said I'd let her know. I could call her and you and I can go over there and see what she has to say. How about it? I've never been to a séance and this might be interesting."

"I don't know, Bill … I personally don't believe in fortune telling. It's a lot of phony superstition, if you ask me. You can go, but leave me out. I think they're nothing but a con game to get your money. Harry Houdini and Sir Arthur Conan Doyle spent the last years of their lives exposing these frauds. They never did find a real spiritualist."

"Yea, I know, I know, but it's just for fun. I've never been to one and I'd like to see what they do."

"Look," I said, "I'm not paying for some fake telling me what I want to hear."

"Okay, don't worry," Bill, said, "it won't cost you a dime. I told you she said it was for free. I guess that was her way of tipping me for the delivering her furniture. It can't hurt anyone, and it won't cost you anything except time. What do you say, George? Let's give it a try."

"Well, okay, if you insist. But remember, I'm not paying her anything."

"We'll go tonight. I'll set it up," Bill said. "You'll see it'll be a lot of fun."

The Fortune Teller

It was a big two-family house with a flat upstairs and one downstairs. We pushed the downstairs bell, but it didn't seem to work. Then, we used a brass knocker shaped like the head of a bull with a large ring through its nose. Finally, a burly shirtless man opened the door. He was over six feet tall and, I'd guess, well over 200 pounds. He looked like he could be a wrestler and we could call him 'The Bone Crusher'.

"What do you want?" he demanded.

Bill and I looked at each other in amazement. I guess Bill hadn't seen this guy when he delivered the furniture. We were about to say "I think we have the wrong house," when a woman's voice came from inside.

"Who's there Waldo?"

Then before he could answer, the voice said, "It's all right, Waldo, it's the furniture delivery man and his friend. Let them in. I've been expecting them."

There wasn't much light in the house and from what I could see Mrs. 'Waldo' was a middle aged woman. Her hair was pinned up in a ball on top of her head, and she was wearing a purple robe. She looked like she was smiling behind her large gold-rimmed glasses. I 'think' she was smiling. It was either a smile or a sneer. It was hard to tell in the poor lighting.

"We came over for the séance, but we can come back some other time when you're not busy," Bill said as we both backed away.

"No, no, come right in," she said, coming to the door. "Waldo, get away from the door and let these nice boys in." The overgrown puppy dog stepped aside and Mrs. Waldo came out to usher us in.

"I've been waiting for you," she said. "Come right into my parlor." She led us into a small room to the left of the vestibule. It also was too dimly lit to see clearly. The room was empty except for about thirty folding chairs circling the wall and on a small table at the far side of the room holding a small lamp, which gave the only illumination. The blinds on the only window were pulled down.

This must be were Mrs. Waldo holds her séances, I thought. What, no crystal ball?

"Take a seat," she said very pleasantly, pointing to the folding chairs. "Take any one of them, please."

We certainly had our choice. Bill and I took two seats together at the opposite end of the room. "Is this all right?" Bill asked.

"That's just fine," she said as she closed the door to the room. "Now, don't be frightened. I'm just going to turn off the light. I cannot communicate with the spirits of the other world and foretell the future with the lights on. I must also have complete silence, or the spirits will leave me." With this, she touched a switch near the door where she was sitting and the room instantly turned pitch black. We were in total darkness. Usually you can see light around the cracks of the door to an outside room, but the vestibule we had come from was itself so poorly lit that nothing came through the cracks in the door. It's a good thing she said don't be afraid, I thought. I wondered what was next on her agenda.

Then we heard a load moan and a screech and some weird noises and garbled talking that didn't make any sense. She must be trying to call the spirits, I thought. Why did I ever let Bill talk me into this mess anyway? I'll be glad when we're out of here!

Speak to me, O spirits," she finally uttered in some understandable tones. "Tell me the future of these two gentlemen." Her voice had changed to a deep guttural sound. "Tell me the secrets and let me look far into the future, O spirits of the outer world. Yes, yes, Bill will prosper and marry a beautiful girl. He will have many children."

Then the tone of her voice seemed to change again and after more indistinguishable sounds and garbled words sounding like a foreign language, she said, "George will marry a beautiful girl and he will prosper and have a house full of children. Both Bill and George will have many blessings." More garbled words that we could not understand. Suddenly she gave a loud screech and shouting "No!" she turned on the light and muttered in her own voice, "I cannot foretell anymore … the spirits have left me … you must go!"

I looked at Bill and stared at the spiritualist. Her head bowed, she seemed upset with her hands over her ears. Suddenly, she sprang to her feet, and opening the door, she said, "You will have to excuse me, gentlemen. Please go. I am tired now. Perhaps some other time I can tell you more of your future." With this, she stepped out into the vestibule and opening the outside door for us, she said, "Go, and read chapter 6, the 20th to the 27th verse of St. Luke in the Holy Bible." With this, she stepped out into the vestibule and opening the outside door for us, she said, "Go! Read chapter 6, the 20th to the 27th verse of St. Luke in the Holy Bible."

Now, that's a switch, I thought. I'm expecting witches and devils and she tells me to read the Bible. Maybe she's a religious nut. The burly Mr. Waldo was nowhere in sight. We were only too glad to get out of there. What a strange and eerie experience. I wonder what made her stop so abruptly?

"What a weird place, and what a nut that dame is," I said as Bill and I entered the car. You don't think that she saw something that she didn't want to talk about? Do you?

"She sure had me wrong, "Bill said. Many kids—-ha! What a laugh."

"What about me? Imagine me having a house full of kids. Now, that's a bigger laugh. I wonder what Marge will say when I tell her that she's going to have a house full of kids."

"Well, this one was free, and that's about all it was worth. I wonder why she stopped so suddenly, Bill mused. "Almost as if she saw something bad that she didn't want to tell us about."

"And, what about the Bible chapter 5 of St. Mathew," I said. "I wonder what that was all about."

"Maybe it says to pay her for her séance. Either that, or she's starting her own church. All you need to start a church these days is the Bible."

"I've heard that sometimes spiritualists mix religion into their séances," I added.

"It sure was different than what I expected," Bill said. "The hollering and screeching, I expected. But I also expected to see some floating horns and ghostly faces. I guess she's not into that yet."

"She really didn't tell us much of anything," I said. "But what do you expect for nothing anyway?"

Blessed Are They

That night when I got home I looked up the 5th chapter of St. Mathew and it turned out to be the Sermon on the Mount. It didn't have any special meaning to me. The next day when I told Marge about this spiritual episode, we both had a good laugh. "Imagine me," Marge said, "having a house full of kids. I like children, but how many is a house full?"

"It depends on how big the house is, I guess," Shaking my head. "Two children—a girl for you and a boy for me. That's my idea of a perfect family. Two is more than enough for anybody."

With that we quickly forgot the whole incident.

IX

LOVE AND MARRIAGE

When a man and woman are married
Their romance ceases and their history commences.
Abbe de Rochebrune 1740-1810

I gave her a diamond engagement ring for Christmas. We planned our wedding for September. We were waiting until September, because I had purchased a new Ford two door in June of 1951 with a year's payments. I would finish my payments on the loan in June of 1952. This gave us a couple months to save some money for our wedding.

On September 6, 1952, we were married at the Holy Redeemer Church. It was a pretty big wedding. Bill was my best man and my brother was an usher. I think that was a mistake. I now am an advocate for family, your brother, as the best man. But when my brother got married a year earlier, he had his best friend as the best man. So be it. We had a nice brunch at the Botsford Inn and we had our honeymoon at Niagara Falls. It was a nice week and the beginning of a new life.

Wedding Day Photo

My Blue Heaven

We had rented a two-bedroom upper flat at 1707 Livernois in Detroit. Like the song *'Tea For Two'* we were in our blue heaven. But Marge wanted children and I thought, okay,—here we go. We had talked about children when the priest was giving us the pre-marital instruction. I remember that Father Peter J. Forbes, pastor of our church telling us, "God's primary purpose of marriage is to bring children into the world. That's why God made man and woman and unites them in the Holy Sacrament of Marriage."

We knew what the Catholic Church taught about the many blessings of a family and we were in agreement about the fun of having a family with children. And it was the idea of our having children that had caused Marge to change her mind and say 'yes'. So there were no surprises. But guess what? After six months of trying, Marge was not pregnant. Now, we were finding that having children was not that easy. Marge asked our doctor.

Why, doctor, can't I become pregnant?

"I'm afraid that you will probably never have any children," he said. "It's your biological makeup. You will probably never be able to conceive. But if it's any consolation to you, there are many people like you. You could adopt a child if you feel you need children."

I was not for adoption. I thought that if God figured that we should not have children, then, that decision was good enough for me. Not having children is another honorable vocation. We could just take more vacations and travel and have fun. Children are expensive and they take up a lot of your time. Not to mention the anxiety and grief that children sometimes give you. No children—that's okay with me, and I think that Marge would go along with this.

But, a month after the doctor's prognosis, Marge became pregnant. It was hard to believe. Another miracle? But with Marge, you never knew what she could do. It reminded me of something I read about old Henry Ford the First having once said, "The difficult, we do immediately; the impossible takes a little longer." I'm told that the Seabees and the Army Engineers also used Ford's statement as their motto. Where Ford got it is a mystery to me.

Baby and Me

Nine months later, the first-born. Mary Ann, named after my mother, was born feet first. "Lucky you came to Ford Hospital for this birth," the nurse said to me when she showed me the baby.

"Ford Hospital is accustomed to these types of births and we're all set up for them. The baby was given a clean bill of health."

Two days later, the doctor told us that the baby was not doing well. Because she was not able to take nourishment from her breast feedings, they thought that there might be an obstruction in her throat. But, the X-rays proved negative. The decision was made to put her on formula and stop the breast feedings. Finally, we were told that all was well again; the baby was doing great on formula and gaining weight.

Taking care of the first baby is not easy for new parents. Baby Mary Ann was just a few months old when she ran a fever. Marge called the doctor. "You must come over to the apartment; our baby has a fever of 101.

"Just bring her to the office," he said.

"Doctor, it's winter and I'm not taking her out in this cold weather. You must come here," Marge said with the righteous determination of a mother protecting her child.

"But Mrs. Arsenault, we do it all the time. The cool air will help bring down her temperature. But if you insist, I'll stop over on my way home."

"I insist!" Marge said.

The doctor made a house call. He left the motor running in his Cadillac with the door wide open as he raced up to our second floor apartment with his little black bag. He gave the baby a shot and went running back down the stairs to his car. It was evident that he was not worried about the health of our baby. Running after him I asked, "How much do I owe you?"

"Twenty dollars."

Hurriedly I pulled a twenty out of my wallet and handed it him. "Will she be all right?"

"Oh sure. If she's not better tomorrow, call me he said as he climbed into his Cadillac."

Baby Mary Ann was better the next day and the second crisis for the new parents was over. The words of a song echoed in my head, *Just Margie and me and baby make three, we're happy in my blue heaven.*

New House

About a year later, Marge was expecting a second baby. When we told the landlady the good news she said, "You know that an apartment is no place to raise children. I'm sorry to tell you, but you will have to move. I'll give you two months to find another place."

So there we were; expecting our second baby and we get our eviction notice. Having read about the houses being built for veterans with the GI Bill for only five hundred dollars down. This was another benefit I received for my service time. We began to look at new houses for GI Veterans. We looked in the city of Livonia and in Allen Park. Because Allen Park was closer to Detroit, where I worked and where my widowed mother lived as well as Marge's parents, we finally bought a new house in a builder's development project in Allen Park. But our house would not be ready for some six to eight months so our second baby, Patrick Joseph, was born on June 23rd of 1955. I knew our landlady would not kick us out, but, I also knew she was right about raising children in cramped quarters not being a good idea. She very kindly said that we could stay until our new house was built which would be sometime in the fall.

Allen Park

We moved to our new Allen Park home where it seemed each year or two the patter of little feet continued until we had a large family of seven children. That's a lot of names to come up with for each baby. What's in a name? All the children's names had various rationales behind them:

The first-born was named Mary Ann after her grandmother Arsenault. Also, the year of 1954 was called the Marian Year by the Catholic Church as a year dedicated to Mary the Mother of Christ. So, it seemed to be appropriate for the year.

The second born in 1955 was Patrick Joseph and named after Marge's brother who was earning his way through the University of Michigan Law School as a cab driver. Also, my father's first name was Joseph.

The third born in 1956 we named Margaret Elizabeth to please Marge's godmother Margaret Elizabeth who was seriously ill at the time. The fourth born in 1958 was named Robert Ernest in memory of my brother who had died so young and my father, who was called Ernest, his second name. The fifth born in 1959 was Mark Anthony in honor of Marge's two favorite saints, St. Mark and St. Anthony.

The sixth born in 1960 was Aileen Therese in honor of Marge's sister Aileen who had died at the age of twenty-one from leukemia a dozen years before. Marge really loved her older sister dearly and had watched her waste away from this dreadful disease. Whenever Marge would speak of her, she always had tears in her eyes.

In eight years we had seven children. But, who's counting and all I know is that Marge wanted a big family and she was happiest and healthiest when she was with her children. I had a good job with GM and we could take care of all of them.

"After your miraculous cure at age thirteen," I would tease her, "the nuns at school told you that you were destined for great things. Well, if they could see you now! You with a house full of kids would surprise them."

"My children are my great things," she would tell me. "My blessings are my children."

"Well," I would answer in jest, "if we have enough of them, maybe one will turn out all right."—Silently praying they all would.

Marge loved her family. She was happiest when she was with them. She had the patience of a saint and the understanding and unselfish love that only a good mother could have. She was quick to praise and slow to find fault. Even her corrections were more of discussion of right and wrong with her children than decrees. She was a teacher and a mother. When she talked to her children, she would also listen to them. The ability to listen that was the key. She treated each one as an individual with his or her own personality. She never tried to dominate them. I was happy to have Marge as the mother of my children.

X

EVENTS

> *Events of all sorts creep and fly exactly as God pleases*
>
> *William Cowper 1731-1800*

In the summer of 1961, Marge began experiencing terrible headaches and earaches. She was beginning to have trouble remembering telephone numbers, even her mother's number. She would go to tears as she struggled to remember.

As weeks went by, her headaches and earaches gradually increased in frequency and severity. Her balance was becoming more impaired and there were indications that not only her memory was diminishing but also her ability to reason and carry on a conversation. Her logic was becoming more and more confused. She would loose track of what day it was, or even what time of the day it was. And when I corrected her on this, she would see her error and go into tears because of her mistakes. She wondered what was happening to her. Her vision began to play tricks on her and sometimes she would see double. All this was happening during the summer of 1961.

At first when the headaches occurred, I thought it was just the normal headache that everyone sometimes gets. I tried not to think about what might be the real reason. The explanation was far more complex than a simple headache and the remedy perhaps far more serious. Still, I grasped at every straw to avoid the conclusion that lingered with me as the only plausible explanation. The symptoms all pointed to a repeat of the symptoms of twenty years ago that indicated a brain tumor. I was hoping that if I ignored what might be reality, maybe it would go away. I remembered somebody saying, "People who are cured by a miracle, never die from what they were cured of." I quickly accepted this—hoping it was true.

I remember the first time I became aware of how severe her headaches were. It was about two o'clock in the morning when she woke me up. "George, you have to go out and get me some aspirins. We're all out and I can't stand this headache."

"What?" I asked, looking at the clock, "at two in the morning, you want me to go out and buy aspirin? Are you kidding? Is the headache that bad?"

"Really bad … and I'm not kidding!" she cried. "You have to go!"

"Of course I'll go." I said as I got out of bed putting my pants on over my pajamas.

Pulling out of my driveway I thought—here it is two in the morning—where am I going to find a drugstore open at this time of the night? I didn't realize how many aspirins she must have been taking to run out like this. I spotted a bar and thought that maybe they would have aspirin. But they had closed at 2 a.m. Then I spotted a restaurant that was open. I went inside and they had little packages of aspirin. I raced home to find Marge waiting at the door.

The next day we went to see our family doctor. After his careful examination, he recommended that we see a neurologist or neurosurgeon. I knew where he was leading us. We made an appointment with Doctor Aaron, who was the protégé of the neurosurgeon Marge had twenty years ago. Her original surgeon had died and Dr. Aaron took over the same office.

By this time, Marge's condition had worsened. Each day seemed to bring new symptoms. She was now dragging her left foot and needed assistance to walk. The doctor gave Marge a careful examination and as I had feared, he diagnosed Marge's trouble as a possible recurrence of her brain tumor. "I'll have to find the original records of the operation of 1942 to see what the prognosis was after the operation," he said.

"Do you think this could get any worse, Doctor?" I asked, hoping for some encouragement.

"One never knows in these cases, but it will be well for us to restudy the original case and go on from there."

"But why ..." I asked. "After twenty years?"

"We don't know. There's much we don't know about the brain. We don't know why a thirteen year old has a brain tumor nor a man at the age of fifty who was in good health has one. What medicine knows about the brain can be put in one book. All we know after some very unpleasant tests is that the tumor is there and that alone. Our only treatment at this time is to attempt to remove the tumor by operating and/or using radiation to shrink the tumor."

"Isn't there any other possible explanation for her symptoms?" I asked.

"Yes, but we'll be able to know more after we see the prognosis notes of the original operation."

"When will that be?"

"This week," he said. "I'll call you."

A week later, Dr. Aaron's nurse called to tell us the doctor had found the records of the original operation and would like to see us.

"Well doctor, what did you find out?" I anxiously asked the doctor while Marge was waiting in the examination room. "Contrary to your belief," the doctor said, "No tumor was removed in the 1942 operation"

"But doctor," I said, "she got better and everyone was under the impression that the operation was a success."

"It was a success, because all the symptoms had disappeared. But you can see here in his notes written immediately after the operation, the doctor states after he opened the area at the back of the head," ... and observed *tissues of insignificance.* I remember Marge telling me that she had had radiation treatments after the operation for any remaining tumor.

"The tumor may still be there," he said. "The radiation treatments were used to shrink the tumor. It is quite apparent that the operation did relieve the pressure in the head and radiation may well have shrunk the tumor. This would account for the remarkable recovery that she did have, but," he continued, pointing to the papers on his desk—" these notes of the doctor clearly indicate that they did not see any tumor. Probably because of the tumor's location being more in the center of the head and it would have been too dangerous to go any deeper. Therefore, after observing 'tissues of insignificance' the procedure was just to close the incision. Her remarkable recovery was otherwise unexplainable. She is a very remarkable girl," he said. "It's her will and determination that has served her well all these years."

"Do you think that this is the same tumor?" I asked.

"I don't know," he said. "I think that we should admit her to the hospital where we can take some tests and then we will be able to tell what it is and what can be done for her. We'll have to play it by ear."

Harper Hospital

Two days later, Marge was admitted into Harper Hospital for tests. I knew that these were serious procedures because every time they did a test, I had to sign a paper to approve the procedure. And these tests always involved the operating room. I found out that in one test, they shaved a spot on the top of her head and drilled a hole to remove fluid and then X-rayed and replaced fluid. Other tests involved inserting dyes and more X-rays. Every day, Marge had another test and every day there was another paper for me to sign.

Testing

Weeks went by and Marge's health in the hospital became progressively worse. I was sure that the tests were taking their toll. You take any healthy person and submit them to the same tests and they wouldn't be feeling too well either. After the first few tests, Marge was unable to get out of bed by herself. She had a wheelchair along side her bed to go to the bathroom and to go to the next test. The only two things that she could do were to smoke and watch TV. She watched all the soap operas every day. It helped to take her mind off her own problems.

One afternoon, when I arrived at the hospital from work, I found Marge in bed with the foot of the bed elevated about three feet higher than the head. "What's going on here," I asked the nurse in charge.

"Marge had a test today that caused her blood pressure to change and the doctor ordered this position for eight hours to prevent her from having severe headaches. We'll be around shortly to lower the foot of the bed."

"How do you feel, Marge?" I asked.

"I'm okay I guess. But will you please light me a cigarette. They won't let me smoke unless someone is with me."

"Is that right?" I said, lighting two cigarettes at a time as in the movies. "Why did they do that?"

"Well, earlier today after one of the tests, I tried to light up and I dropped the match. The bed sheets caught fire and I yelled as I tried to pat the fire out. The result was just a little burn hole. But now I can't smoke alone."

"Did you get any burns?"

"No, just scared. My balance and coordination aren't what they use to be."

"I know. I'm glad it wasn't any worse than that. Maybe it is better that you don't smoke unless someone is here to help you.

"Did the doctor come in to see you today?" I asked.

"He never fails."

"What did he say? Anything new?"

"Not really. He just said that he would be talking to you as soon as all the tests are completed."

"I'll give him a call tomorrow."

Operation

The next morning, when I called him on the phone, the doctor told me that they needed another test before he could make any diagnosis. That night after work when I went to the hospital, I found Marge resting comfortably, but none the better.

Another week went by and the tests were completed and the results were in. The X-ray specialists had made their report. The labs had all finalized their reports and the time was here for the doctor's analysis and decision for the course of action. I did not really want to hear it when the doctor called me aside at the hospital and said, "There are no indications of a brain tumor in the original area at the base of the head. However, this time our tests indicate that there is a tumor in the frontal right lobe area."

"Does this mean another operation?"

"I'm afraid we have no alternative," he said. "Her condition is deteriorating and the best way to handle this is to operate immediately and remove the tumor. This time we will be able to see the tumor and the prognosis is good. Also, she is young and that is in her favor. We can hope for a complete recovery if the tumor is not malignant. She has a good chance that it is not malignant based on her history of the prior tumor."

"What are our chances, doctor?" I forced myself to ask.

"Very good for this condition. I'd say fifty-fifty."

That didn't sound very good to me—fifty-fifty. I passed the word at home to the children and told them to pray for their mother. I also called St. Mary Magdalene School and asked the principal, Sister Janet, and the good nuns to remember Marge in their prayers. I sent a telegram to Father Methodius (Dick Telnack) with whom

I had graduated from Holy Redeemer High School and who now was a Trappist monk at Our Lady of the Holy Spirit Monastery in Conyers, Georgia. I figured that he had a direct line to the Lord. The telegram read:

> Father Methodius
> Marge scheduled for a brain-tumor operation.
> Doctors give her a fifty-fifty chance.
> Need prayers! George Arsenault

Dick Telnack was the smartest guy in my high school class. In 1946, when we graduated, we were in line to be drafted into the army. So, as I had stated earlier, Dick enlisted in the Marines for two years and I enlisted in the Army for eighteen months. After he got out of the Marines, he joined the Trappist monks, fed up with the way the world was going, I guessed, he took the bull by the horns and joined the Trappist. He's only a little guy, but to me, he's a giant among men. I had already written to him about Marge and I felt that he could help with his prayers. I thought to myself, when all else fails—try prayer. It's strange how we ask God to understand our plans and us yet and we give little thought to understanding God and His plans.

Is there really power in prayer? I asked myself. It's times like this that we want to believe. Didn't Christ say, "If you have the faith of a mustard seed, you can move mountains." and "If you ask the Father for anything in my name, He will give it to you. Ask and you shall receive. Seek and you shall find. Knock and it shall be opened unto you." These were the words I needed to keep telling myself.

Success

The operation was scheduled for eight in the morning of Halloween, the day before All Saints Day. If we ever needed all saints, it was today, I thought as I drove to the hospital at about 6am. It was the old army game, hurry up and wait. After the surgery, the doctor appeared in the doorway of the waiting room and motioned for me to come out in the hallway.

"How is Marge?" I anxiously asked.

"She's fine," he said. "We were able to remove about ninety percent of the tumor. It was the size of an orange. We just kept taking off a little at a time until bit by bit we had most of it. We kept her semi-conscious in order for her to help us identify the area we were working on. It is amazing that with this size tumor, she was able to function as well as she had. Also amazing was when she was taken to the recovery room she asked for a glass of water and she surprised us all when she took the glass and lifting it directly to her mouth, she drank from it. She couldn't do that before the operation, you know. It's almost miraculous"

"When will I be able to see her?"

"In about an hour they'll be returning her to her room. You can see her then."

She was lying in bed with her head completely bandaged. She was looking up at me and smiling, "Hi honey."

"Hi," I said. "How are you feeling?"

"Okay, I guess," she said. "I've got a little headache and I feel weak, but outside of that I'm okay."

"The doctor said you were great during the operation and the operation was a success. You'll be coming home in a few days," I said wiping a tear from the corner of my eye.

"The operation wasn't so bad," she said. "It was easier than delivering a baby."

"Well, the worst is over and as Shakespeare said, '*all's well that ends well …*' and Amen."

The next day, when I arrived at the hospital after work at about suppertime, I did not find Marge in her room. I went to the nurse's station. "Where is my wife, Margaret Arsenault? She's not in her room. Did something go wrong?"

"No, Mr. Arsenault, nothing went wrong," a nurse said. "I think that you will find her having a cigarette in the visitor's lounge."

"You have to be kidding," I said. "That's a lot of trouble for you people to wheel her down to the visitor's lounge just to have a cigarette."

When I arrived there, I found Marge sitting up in a chair just as pretty as a picture and smoking her cigarette. She smiled when she saw me and said, "Hi honey, are you surprised?"

"Surprised?" I stuttered. "I'm amazed. Where is the nurse? And where is your wheelchair?"

"The nurse is around somewhere and I didn't need a wheelchair. I walked here with the nurse. I wanted to surprise you," she said.

"Surprise me? You astounded me," I said. "I must be dreaming. I can't believe it. Two days ago you couldn't go anywhere without a wheelchair. Today, you're walking. Here we go again … another miracle. You amaze me."

She walked back to her room, arm in arm, with me. She hadn't walked in six weeks. Our prayers were answered, I thought. The doctor said she would go home in a few days and he was right.

I found out that prayers were said by all the parish school children every day for the past six weeks that she had been in the hospital. The principal, Sister Janet asked for prayers every day over the loudspeaker. Sister Janet's and the Mother Superior, Sister Frances' requests for prayers by the Saint Mary Magdalene Parochial school children and the prayers of Father Methodius plus all of our family had paid off. All of my five oldest children and the school had been praying every day for Marge's recovery.

Marge was coming home. This was another of her miracles. She was a fighter from the word go. She now could be with her children who were not allowed to visit her in the hospital for over a month.

Janet Frances

Was Marge all right after this second brain tumor operation at the age of thirty-two? Outside of the fact that she had to grow a new head of hair, she was better than all right. In fact, a year later in 1962, we were waiting for the birth of a new baby. The baby would be a cesarean birth, as the doctors had advised for her last three babies. The doctor had picked November 9 as the delivery date. But that was the day my dad had died and my mother suggested that the baby be born on a different day. So, the doctor said, "No problem, we'll just make it November 8."

So, on November 8, Marge delivered a beautiful new healthy little baby girl. We named her Janet Frances for the two nuns that had prayed for Marge's recovery the prior year. Our family now numbered seven children: four girls and three boys.

Seven Arsenault Children—1962

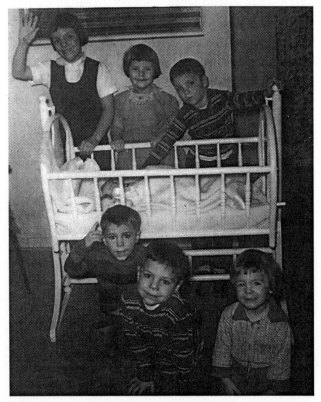

Seven Arsenault Children
Back Row: Mary Ann, Margaret Elizabeth, Patrick Joseph
Crib: Janet Frances
Front Row: Mark Anthony, Robert Ernest, Aileen Therese

XI

ADVERSITY

The flower that follows the sun does so even on cloudy days.
-Robert Leighton 1611-1684.

With all our past troubles, the world went on its own way unmindful of my own problems. The year is 1963. In June, Pope John XXIII died. In August, the 'hot line' between Washington and Moscow began operation. September 21, President John Kennedy announced that he was sending Defense Secretary Robert McNamara and the Chairman of the Joint Chiefs of Staff, General Maxwell Taylor, to South Vietnam to review our military effort.

October 1 was a beautiful fall day in Michigan. I was on my way home from work—only a few blocks from home—when, hearing a siren blaring, I pulled my car to the side of the road as an ambulance sped by me with its lights flashing.

The way he's driving and the direction he's going, I thought, he must be headed for Outer Drive Hospital with someone in deep trouble.

Years ago—at Holy Redeemer Catholic School—the nuns told us, "whenever you hear a siren, say a prayer for somebody in trouble." I guess there are some things from out of our past that we never forget.

I was turning the corner of our street, when I spotted a group of neighbors in front of our house. I pulled over to the curb. As I got out of my car, I heard someone say, "There's the father."

Oh—oh … what's happening here? I hesitatingly thought and thinking to myself, do they mean me? I'm the father they want?

John, my next-door neighbor came up to me. "George, there's been an accident. The ambulance just left with Marge. You must have just passed it. Go to Outer Drive Hospital—hurry!"

A uniformed police officer came over. "Your wife has been burned. Your neighbors are looking after your children. So, I think you had better go direct to the Emergency Room at the Outer Drive Hospital."

I hadn't even noticed the police car across the street. Now its flashing red lights added to my apprehension of misfortune.

A cold sweat popped out on my forehead. "Are my children all right?"

"The children are fine." John said pointing towards our house. "Ira (his wife) is with them. You'd better get to the hospital right away. Don't worry about the children - - - we'll take care of them until you get back. Just go!"

Outer Drive Hospital

At the hospital, I found Marge in the hallway of the Emergency Room sitting upright on a chair. She had a white sheet wrapped around her shoulders. She was fully conscious.

Seeing me, she said in a whisper, "Don't touch me. I'm burned from my neck down to my waist."

"What happened Marge?" I asked with tears in my eyes.

"This is probably the dumbest thing I've ever done," she said. "I was cooking supper and I had on my new blouse and sweater you just bought me from Hudson's. When I turned, I must have been too close to the gas stove and the next thing I knew, my blouse and sweater were on fire. I ran outside screaming for help when Ira, next door, heard me and came running over. By the time she got there, my blouse and sweater already had burned itself out. Some of the neighbors put this sheet around me and somebody brought me a chair to sit on."

"You must be in terrible pain," I said. "Have they given you anything for pain?"

"Yes, they gave me a shot of something. I only feel pain in my arms and neck and some pain on my chest."

"Why are you sitting in a chair? Shouldn't you be lying down?" But then, I thought, how could she lie down with those burns?

"They don't want me to lie down. They said my back was the most seriously burned and that lying down would make it even worse."

"Were you able to sign in and give them the information they needed?"

"Yes, I had to."

"Have they called Dr. Leonard (our family doctor)?"

"Yes. He's on his way with a burn specialist now."

"I think I saw the ambulance you came in. It passed me on my way home from work."

"They had to call two ambulances. The first ambulance did not have a seat for me to sit on and I couldn't lie down. So, they called a van type ambulance where I could sit on a wheelchair."

"The doctors are here now." A nurse approached. "We'll be taking your wife up to her room now, Mr. Arsenault. If you will step over to the desk, they will complete the papers and tell you her room number."

"Keep a stiff upper lip, Marge," I said trying to encourage her. "I love you, Marge and I'll see you in a few minutes." I turned and quickly walked to the emergency desk.

Third Degree

As I pushed open the door to Marge's room, I heard the burn specialist and our doctor talking to her.

"Can you feel anything?" the specialist asked as he placed his two fingers on the raw skin of her back.

"No," Marge said.

"How about this, how does this feel?" the doctor asked, as he touched all around her back.

"No," Marge answered.

"Can you feel this?" as he touched her arms and neck.

"Yes, that hurts," Marge, said.

"Does it hurt only when I touch it?"

"No, it hurts the same."

"I'm going to be frank with you, Marge," the specialist said. "You're badly burned and it will take a long time to heal. But you were lucky that you didn't get burned on your face and that your hair didn't catch fire."

The doctor motioned me toward the door. "Marge, I'll be just outside," I said as I walked to the door.

"I'll be right back."

In the hall, the doctor said, "Your wife has a forty percent burn area. Much of it is third degree burn and that will require skin grafting. Our biggest problem now will be to avoid infection."

"But … why isn't she in more pain … and complaining more?" I asked.

"Part of it is the shock effect to the nerve system. And remember we have her under medication to control pain and shock. Also, when you have third-degree burns, you've destroyed all the nerve cells in the area and there is no pain when the nerve cells are dead. If you feel pain, it will heal. If you don't feel pain, it will not heal by itself."

"How much are third degree burns?" I persisted.

"We know it's her entire back. We don't know how deep. We'll just have to wait and see. What will not heal will be third-degree burns. But our first worry is infection. If we can beat that and get most of the burns healed, then we can think about skin grafts. Infection is always the enemy because a third-degree burn is an open wound that does not heal."

Recuperation

It was now apparent that Marge would be hospitalized for many months. My mother took our 1 year old, Janet and our 3 year old, Aileen. I hired a nanny to watch over the other five children when they came home from school and to see that they were fed. I wanted the children to have good meals and I would 'catch as catch can.' Daily, I would go to work at 7:30 am. After work, I would stop at the hospital for a few minutes to check on Marge. Then, I would go home to check on the rest of the family. Mark, the 5 year old, was in kindergarten. Robert, who was 6, was in first grade. Margaret, 8 year old, was in third grade. Patrick, 9 years old, was in the forth grade and ten year old Mary Ann was in the Fifth grade. Many days, I would get a baby sitter in the evenings and go to the hospital. The days of October were filled with these maneuvers.

In November, the specialist brought in a therapist trained in bathing burn patients. The therapist explained that it would take weeks of careful bathing of Marge's burns to help her fight infection and heal what was healable.

"She will sit in a special chair and we will lower her in a specially medicated tub of warm water," he said. "Daily baths will speed up the healing process and help fight against any infection."

The baths started. Every day they lowered Marge into a tub of warm water. Marge told me that the water would turn red by the time they raised her out of it.

"I bet that really hurts," I said.

"Worse then anything I've ever had!" she said. "Sometimes, I think I'd rather jump out of that window. But then I think of you and the children ... and I would never do that."

"No, don't you ever do that."

"Oh, I know, I know. I won't. I think of you and the children and that helps. And I pray a lot. That helps. I wish I knew the Stations of the Cross for this rosary."

"Maybe I should talk to the doctor about these baths."

"No, don't," Marge, said. "They're all very kind and gentle. They're just doing everything that they can for me. But now that you mention it, please pick up a carton of Viceroys for the therapist. I know that's what he smokes. He's been so nice to me."

Healing

November 22nd, the TV and the radio are all talking about the assassination of President John F. Kennedy in Texas. As I drove routinely from work to the hospital, all the stations on the radio were saying the same: "Our 47 year old President, John F. Kennedy, was fatally shot while riding in a motorcade through Dallas, Texas today."

"Marge," I said as I turned on the television in her room. "The President has been shot."

"Yes, I know. Turn that damn TV off! Spare me the details," she snapped.

"The bath pain must have really been bad today," I said as I turned off the TV.

"It was ... and the water is still turning red. I've got enough trouble now and I don't have the patience to listen to someone else's agony."

"I know it's painful, but the baths must be working. You've avoided infection—and see: a lot of your burns have already healed."

"Oh sure. But it still hurts like hell—every damn day."

"Well, don't give up," I said. "Keep up the fight. We'll get out of this thing yet. I promise."

"That's easy for you to say, you don't have to bear the pain. But don't worry. I've gone this far. I can go the rest of the way."

"Good for you," I said. "Everyone's praying for you. The kids ... all of St. Mary Magdalene Grade School are saying a prayer for you every day."

Because most of the burn areas were left uncovered and loose gauze just barely covered the rest, I could see that at least half the burns were healing. But her back still looked raw. As the doctors had said, most of her back had third degree burns. Skin grafting operation is next, I thought.

I was right. On December the first, the doctors told us of their plans.

"Marge," the doctor said, "we would like to schedule a skin graft operation for the last day of the year. We will attempt to graft skin from your legs to all the third degree area of your back in this one operation. If we are successful, you can start the new year right." He looked from Marge to me. "We want Marge to quit smoking as soon as possible so as to clear the blood stream of constricting nicotine. This will enhance the body's ability to successfully take the grafting and healing process. That way we can hope for less grafting needed at a later date if any at all."

"We can do that ... right Marge?" I said.

"What do you mean ... 'We'?"

"I'll quit with you, Marge. Everyone should quit anyway."

"Well, I guess I can quit if I have to."

"Sure you can. We can do it together."

"By the way Doc, will Marge be able to come home for a couple days for Christmas?" I said.

"We'll see if we can arrange a furlough for her."

XII

SMOKING

> *Man is, properly speaking, based upon hope; he has no other possession but hope; this world of his is emphatically the place of hope.*
>
> —*Alexander Carlyle 1748-1825*

I bought every book I could find on how to quit smoking. The Surgeon General of the United States had just that year declared that smoking can cause cancer, so there were a lot of books out on the subject. I recall '*How to Quit Smoking Or Double Your Money Back*' and '*Smoking Is For Suckers*'. Another was a medical review with graphic pictures of lungs and vivid stories about the slow strangulation of emphysema, heart trouble and mouth and throat cancer. Ugh! I just skimmed though that one. It wasn't going to be easy for two people like Marge and me who each smoked a pack or more a day, to quit cold. But all the books suggested cold turkey was the best way. Even though we both smoked like chimneys, Marge and I agreed that we should go cold turkey. In addition to saving money, we would both improve our health, and Marge's upcoming skin grafts would have a better chance for success.

December 8th was the date we chose for cold turkey. I bought 2 one-dollar cigars the night before my farewell to smoking. My mouth was like a furnace as I smoked one cigar after another. I had a burnt taste in my mouth. That'll teach me, I thought. I discovered that the first twenty-four hours are the worst. It takes that long to get the nicotine out of your blood stream. And, it takes about two weeks to get it out of your other systems. I believe I read that it takes five years to clear out your lungs alone. The book experts had suggested substituting another habit to take the place of smoking. I chose salted pumpkin seeds. Marge chose gum. Whenever we had the urge for a cigarette—which was all the time—we would be chewing gum, or eating pumpkin seeds instead of smoking.

When I awoke on the morning of the eighth; I had been off cigarettes for eight hours. But all day I kept reaching my shirt pocket for a cigarette. As the book had suggested, I didn't tell anyone that we had quit smoking. I thought to myself smugly, look at them, acting like nothing is wrong. They don't even know that I haven't had a cigarette all day. People offered me cigarettes and didn't even ask questions when I said "no thanks."

"Well, Marge, did you stop smoking?" was the first question I asked when I got to her room.

"I've done pretty good," she said. "I only had two cigarettes all day."

"What's good about that? I've had none, zero, cold-turkey remember our agreement?"

"Oh, I remember. But it's not easy."

"Yes, I know it's not easy. But it'll get easier the longer you stay away from them," I said as I tried to persuade and encourage her. "That's what the books say. It's really a matter of memory. When you first quit, you remember every minute that you're not smoking and you are aware every minute that you're not smoking. You will watch others light up and find yourself reaching for a cigarette. But as time goes by, there are minutes that you forget that you're not smoking. And I guess these minutes will lapse into hours as days go by. After a few weeks, these hours of forgetting that you're not smoking will lengthen into days. When that happens, we've got it licked. We'll finally have that smoke monkey off our backs. Alleluia. If it's not cold turkey, it's just a prolonged agony so I'm told.

"OK, OK, cold-turkey. If you can do it, I guess I can too."

"I know you can and I know that it's hard to quit. Remember my quitting for twenty-four hours the first day of Lent every year for Lenten penance? That was agony. I can remember waiting for the clock to hit midnight at the end of that day. Remember how I would have a match lit and the cigarette in my mouth waiting for that first puff? What a slave I was to tobacco. So I knew the first day would be bad. But today is a tiny bit easier."

Christmas

Marge came home two days before Christmas. The house was filled with Christmas cheer. The children were elated. Although she could not wear any dresses and still had these loose bandages around her, we had two happy days with Marge home again and running her household. She still could not lie on her back and had to sleep on her side. But after three long months without her children (the hospitals did not allow children to visit), Marge was back home for a few days with her children. The children happily waited on her and Mary Ann, our ten year old, was at her beck and call.

On December the 30th, grafting took place on her back. Two strips of about one inch wide and eight inches long were taken from the upper thigh of each leg and placed across Marge's back. When I saw her after the operation, not only her torso but both upper legs were bandaged.

"How do you feel?" I asked her when they finally let me in the room.

"Good!" she said. "When they put me out, all the pain went away. It was the first time in three months that finally I was able to get some rest."

"Well, at least that's a plus."

"Did you talk with the doctors?" she asked.

"Yes. They said the operation went very well. They think that with a little luck this one operation may be all you will need. Now, that's really good news."

"One operation is all I want," Marge said. "But what I really want is my walking papers so I can get out of here and go home."

I remember the radio singing, "I Love you because", "I Want To Be Around", and Tony Bennett was singing "The Good Life". Even Richard Chamberlain, TV's Dr. Kildare was singing "All I Have To Do Is Dream". On this last day of 1963 we were looking forward to 1964 as a better year for all of us.

Routine

As the weeks went by, I developed a routine. I would see the kids off to school in the morning before going to work. I would work till four and go right to the hospital from work to see Marge. During the weekdays I had hired a nanny to feed them and tidy up the house. I also had a local teenager to baby-sit and look after the kids from time to time. My widowed mother took baby Janet to live at her house. On weekends, my mother and the baby would stay at our house. I didn't eat at home except for a late bite. I lost fifteen pounds during these months of running to the hospital. I would normally get back home about six thirty or seven in the evening. I had discovered another way to loss weight—have a tragedy.

Winning

The last week in January, I was with Marge in the hospital during her suppertime at about five o'clock. This had been my usual routine these past four months. Marge was sitting in a chair. The bandages had finally been removed and I could see for the first time the tops of her legs where the skin graft had been taken—both legs they were blood red. I was amazed that they would remove the bandage so soon. I surmised that the doctors must want the air to get to them to help the healing.

"Marge … your legs … look how red they are! They must hurt like hell. They look like they're inflamed. I wonder if they took the bandages off too soon?"

"They're almost all healed," Marge said. "The doctors said that the redness would eventually fade away."

"They don't look healed to me …"

"Well, they are. Go ahead and touch them. You'll see."

I touched the top of her legs. They felt just as smooth as a baby's skin. "I'm amazed," I said. "I'm glad that they're doing well. I was told that they just take only the top layer of skin—like tissue paper—and that they graft it to the burned area and it grows new skin. It's like planting seeds. Pretty neat."

"I guess that's the way it works. They're pretty smart."

"I was told that the doctors gave you a good report this morning. All the skin graft is taking—is this true?"

"I guess it is. They put me on special medication to help prevent infection."

"Well, I sure hope that it does the trick."

"Me too. Did you ask them when I'm getting out of here? My back is better and I don't have bandages any more."

"They tell me that it'll be after they're sure that you will not get any infections on the wounds. They have to keep a close eye on you—but I'm sure it will be soon. I think we're winning!

Her back was getting better. The nurses were applying cocoa butter and that made it feel better. Marge just loved it when the nurses spread cocoa butter over her back each day.

On January 15, 1964, the doctors declare Marge's skin graft operation a huge success. "Marge will not require any more skin graft surgery," the doctor said. Alleluia!

Home Again

The second week in February, Marge was given her long awaited walking papers and officially discharged from Outer Drive Hospital after five long months. I was able to hire a housekeeper to help Marge for five days a week. Marge was home but she could not do very much. It was difficult for her to walk and she still needed help to get her strength back. We had a full house. In our three-bedroom ranch home, I had built two rooms in the basement (our lower level) with a bathroom for the three boys. The two oldest girls were in one bedroom, the two youngest were in the other and Marge and I were in another. The weeks went by and Marge seemed to be getting stronger.

Relapse

It was the seventeenth of March—St. Patrick's Day—when I heard a thud. I had just gone down the basement to check on the boys. Marge had just finished saying good-bye to the housekeeper for the day and had gone to the bedroom to lie down. I raced up the stairs looking for Marge. As I entered the bedroom, I saw her lying next to the bed, a small cut on her forehead.

She was unconscious. She must have passed out and hit her head on the bed as she fell to the floor, I thought. Quick, I said to myself, call the doctor at his office. Maybe he's still in.

"Put a cold cloth on her forehead and stay with her," the doctor said over the phone. "If she doesn't come to in ten or fifteen minutes, have an ambulance take her to Outer Drive Hospital. Have them call me from there."

I had put Marge in the bed and I sat there talking to her. "Marge, wake up. Are you OK? Please wake up, Marge." I kept looking at my watch. After fifteen minutes, I called the ambulance.

XIII

TROUBLE

When troubles comes from God, then naught behooves like patience; but for troubles wrought of me, patience is hard—I tell you it is hard.—Jean Ingelow 1820-97..

At Outer Drive hospital, Marge was still unconscious. "Will she be all right, doctor?" I asked.

"I think so," he said. "We've given her a shot and now we'll have to wait until she comes around. After she's awake for a while, you may be able to take her back home."

Two hours later and Marge was still out. Our family doctor had arrived. He had a worried look on his face when he came over to talk to me. "I'm admitting Marge into the hospital."

"Why isn't she waking up, Doc?"

"I don't know. But I suspect that these past few months have been very hard on her and her old problems may be coming back. You know that she blacked out in the hospital two weeks before we released her."

"No, I didn't know that."

"You better go home to your children. You can't help Marge here," he said. "She's in good hands now. Call me in the morning."

"Thanks Doc. I guess you're right."

"Don't worry," he said. "She'll be better in the morning."

That night I called my mother and brought her to our house to look after the children for the weekend.

Next morning I raced to the hospital. Marge was better. At least she was conscious. "Hi Marge, how's it going?"

"Hi," she said. "I'm feeling weak. I don't know what happened to me."

"I found you unconscious on the floor in the bedroom. I was really worried about you when you wouldn't wake up. But you're in good hands now. The staff remembers you from the burns. They really like you and I know that they'll take good care of you."

"I don't remember a thing until I woke up here. I guess I fainted at home and you brought me here. Do I have to get new walking-papers to go home again?"

"We'll ask the doctor as soon as I see him. He's around here somewhere." Just as I said that, the doctor came into the room.

"Well, our patient is a little better than when she got here last night. Will you excuse us Marge, while I talk to your husband," he said as he motioned me into the hall.

As soon as we were in the hall, he said, "We're going to keep her for a few days. We're treating her for a high fever. I don't know what is causing the fever and I don't want her to catch pneumonia. We're giving her antibiotics."

"She says she's very weak," I said.

"I'm going to call her neurosurgeon, Dr. Aaron, for his opinion. This problem may be related to his area of expertise. She needs rest so don't stay too long. I'll talk to you tomorrow after I have spoken to Dr. Aaron."

The next day Marge seemed better. At least her voice seemed a little stronger. I saw the doctor at the nurses' station.

"Hi Doc," I said. "Did you talk to Doctor Aaron?"

"Yes, and he concurred with my diagnosis. So we decided that it would be better if Marge is transferred to Harper Hospital where Dr. Aaron will take over her care."

"The next morning, I was at the hospital when the ambulance came to transfer Marge to Harper Hospital.

"You're going for a ride today," I said to Marge as they wheeled her down the hall to the ambulance.

"I can use a ride," she said. "This time, maybe I can see some sights."

I followed the ambulance out of the parking lot. When, they turned on their siren and flashing lights, I knew I would never be able to keep up with them, so I didn't even try. By the time I arrived at Harper Hospital, parked the car and found her room, the nurses had already given Marge an alcohol rubdown.

Marge was getting first class treatment. I was glad. I knew that no matter where Marge went, Marge would capture the hearts of all around her as long as she could talk. She just had a way with people and knew how to talk to them. I think that it was the way she would empathize with them. Everyone loved her. After visiting with her, I felt that she was already better then she had been at Outer Drive Hospital. The drive had done her some good.

I went home to check on the children then returned to the hospital around Marge's suppertime. As I walked from the parking lot, I passed a young street vendor who was selling bunches of red roses out of his old beat-up-car in front of the hospital.

"Buy your best girl some roses," he said. "Only five dollars."

"Not today, but save me a dozen later for my best girl."

"I sure will," he said. "Maybe tomorrow?"

"Maybe."

Coincidence, I thought. Then I remembered: in route to the hospital I had heard on my car radio, "*I want some red roses for a blue lady*' so, I turned to the vendor. "On second thought, give me a dozen roses for my best girl right now." And I handed him a five-dollar bill.

"Now you're talking," he said as he handed me a bouquet of red roses. Dr. Aaron was in the hall outside of Marge's room.

"How's my best girl, Doc?" I asked.

"She's very thin and very weak," he said. "We'll have to try to put some weight on her and build up her strength."

"She likes malted milks," I said. "I've been giving her malted milks every day at home for the past month and she really likes them."

"Fine," he said. "Anything that will put weight on her will be fine. We will be putting her on a special diet for that."

So everyday, I brought Marge a special malted milk that I made at home. I had bought a real malt mixer and I was even putting an egg in it. After a week, she seemed to be getting a little stronger and she was even walking a little.

After another week, it was April. Marge was still very weak. I was on my way to her room when I heard someone call "Mr. Arsenault, Mr. Arsenault." Looking around, I saw a nurse waving at me to come over to the nurses' station.

"You're Margaret Arsenault's husband?"

"Yes."

"Your wife is very ill. She has a Staph pneumonia with a high fever. We have given her medication and she is sleeping now. Please try not to disturb her and don't stay too long. Also, Dr. Aaron wants you to call him at his office tomorrow morning."

The next day, the doctor told me over the phone that Marge had Staph pneumonia and they'd had to transfer her to a private room because that type of pneumonia is very infectious.

When I saw Marge later that day, she was really down. I realized that she was in an isolation ward. I had to wear special white robes and a mask to go into her room. "The doctor's say you have Staph pneumonia and they want to do a tracheotomy to help clear your lungs." Marge started to cry. I said, "Marge, it will be all right, they said it will help you."

Well, they had really done it this time. They had taken her roommate and kind nurses away from her and now, anyone she saw would be wearing a mask. She had always enjoyed having someone to talk to in her room. I think that Marge knew more then I did about what a tracheotomy was and the consequences. Dumb as I was, I should have realized that when they wanted me to sign for it, it must have been serious. I should have asked more questions. I should have stalled more before I signed that paper. Her neurosurgeon had said that it was to make it easier for the lung therapist and not his idea.

The next day, I found Marge in an oxygen tent. She opened her eyes and seemed to smile. She couldn't say anything. I discovered that with a tracheotomy, you couldn't talk because they put a hole in your throat for you to breath through. And when they use the suction hose to clear the fluid from your lungs, they have to go through that hole. Now, they've even managed to take her voice away from her, I thought.

That night, I got a call from my mother. "George," she said. "Baby Janet is very sick. We took her to the doctor and he put her in Providence hospital. He said she has Staph pneumonia."

My brother had taken my mother and the baby to the doctor because of a high fever. I called a baby-sitter, and then headed for Providence Hospital in Detroit. It was a thirty-minute drive from Allen Park.

Providence Hospital was on West Grand Boulevard, about fifteen minutes from Harper Hospital. I found baby Janet in a room by herself. She too was in an oxygen tent. She had an intravenous needle in her foot. That's strange, I thought. They were giving her something through the foot. I've never seen that before. Out in the hall, I found the doctor. "How my baby Janet?" I asked.

"You have a very sick baby, Mr. Arsenault," he said. "She has Staph pneumonia and to make matters worse, she's very anemic, which probably explains why she became infected. But, we got her just in time, I think. Tell me, is she a bottle baby?"

"Yes, I think she is," I said. "She loves her bottle."

"Well, it's time to take her bottle away from her. Any fourteen month old baby should have been on solid food long ago."

"Janet has been staying at my mother's house," I told him. "My wife, Margaret, is also in the hospital, at Harper's. She has Staph pneumonia and is in an oxygen tent and she has other complications." I went on to explain Marge's problems and he said, "You certainly have your hands full."

I sure do, I thought. As if one isn't enough, now I have to worry about two. It may have been my fault. I had probably carried that Staph germ inadvertently to Janet in her weakened anemic condition. Maybe in those plastic malted milk containers that I carted back and forth every day from Harper Hospital for Marge's milk shakes.

XIV

Two Hospitals

> With the fearful strain that is on me night and day,
> If I did not laugh, I should die. Abe Lincoln—1809-65

Every day from then on, I would first go to see Janet. I left work at four o'clock and got to Providence around five. I would stay about fifteen or twenty minutes then go to Harper hospital, another ten miles, to see Marge. Marge wasn't getting any stronger. She seemed to be sleeping most of the time. I would have to wake her up each day when I got there. "Marge!" She opened her eyes and seeing me, she would smile.

"Marge, baby Janet is in Providence hospital and she too has Staph pneumonia and is in an oxygen tent."

Marge looked away.

"I want both of you to get out of these oxygen tents," I said.

Marge closed her eyes. I'm not sure she even heard what I said. She still had that hole in her neck and she couldn't talk to me so it was a one-way street.

Janet Frances

Two weeks went by and low and behold, they both were out of the oxygen tents. Janet was eating from a plate and drinking from a glass. What a change! I would help feed Janet with a spoon. She even had regular food, like fish and chicken. She was doing very well and when I visited her each day, she would smile and laugh. But, when I left the room, she would cry. So I started to play a little game with her. I would go out the door, and she would start crying and I would pop back in and say boo. She would stop crying and laugh. I would do this several times and when she was laughing I would leave to go to Harper hospital to see her mother.

Janet was discharged from the hospital the last week in April. She went back to my mother's house with new feeding instructions. Marge, still unable to walk, was still being feed intravenously. I prayed that Marge too would soon be discharged. I prayed that in May, she would come home. Every day, on my way to the hospital, I would say the rosary as fast as I could so I would say as many as possible in that short time. I stopped off at St Patrick's Church near the hospital to light a candle and pray for Marge. The church was mostly empty and I would have to hide my face on my way out with my handkerchief to hide the tears streaming down my face. I sure felt sorry for myself.

Red Roses

On May 26th, I sat with her, not speaking, I was just glad to be there with her in the event she would wake up. At the end of my daily visit, I bent over her and said, "Marge, keep up the fight!"

She opened her eyes and tried to speak. I had learned that if I put my finger over the silver washer in her throat, she could utter some sounds. So I put my finger on the hole and with my ear near her, I was able to discern her saying in a low raspy voice, "keep up the fight when you're hardest hit."

My mind flashed back to an old anonymous poem that we both had known—*Keep up the fight when you're hardest hit; it's when things seem worst that you mustn't quit.* She was trying to tell me that she was hardest hit and things were worse. She closed her eyes and fell back to sleep.

The following day, her eyes remained closed. All this sleeping was probably medication. I wondered if it was necessary.

The next day, the 28th of May, I got a call from Dr. Aaron at my accounting office.

"Mr. Arsenault, you had better come to the hospital right away."

"What's wrong, Doc. Is Marge worse?"

"Yes, I'm afraid so."

"You mean I should leave right now?"

"Right now! You'd better hurry. I'm afraid we're going to lose her."

"I'll be right there!"

I called my mother and her parents and told them what the doctor had said and I left for the hospital as fast as I could.

When I arrived at Marge's room. She wasn't there. They must have moved her again, I thought. I discovered that they had transferred her to the Maternity section. Very appropriate, I thought. She should feel at home there after giving birth to seven children. I'll bet this was the only place that had a vacant room and they didn't want her to die in the section where all the nurses knew and loved her so well.

Marge was in an oxygen tent with all kinds of tubes and machines around her. I reached into the tent for her hand. It was cold. But I could still see her breathing though her eyes were closed. I then went out into the hall. Marge's parents and her brother, Patrick, and her sister, Mary, were in the waiting room down the hall. We paced the floor for about two hours quietly. Finally I said, "Why are we all waiting here?" No one answered me. I knew why we were all waiting and they knew too. We were waiting for Marge to die, but no one had the heart to say it. I certainly would never say it.

"Then why don't you all go home," I finally said. "I'll let you know if anything happens." I felt that they were relieved.

"Be sure and call us immediately if anything happens, or if you need something."

"Of course," I said.

Then they all left. I didn't think that they all would leave. I was alone but I felt better. I was alone with my own agony. I went into Marge's room. She seemed to be having difficulty breathing and her hand was turning bluish. I pushed the aid button. The nurse came in immediately, took one look and said, "Oh my god, I'll get the doctor," and left the room.

I knew what the nurse meant. This was the event we all had been waiting for and now was the time Marge would leave us. I decided to leave too. I went to the elevator across the hall and down to the main floor. I went outside, hoping to get some fresh air and clear my head.

I saw the flower vendor, still there, standing near the curb.

"Red roses for your best girl," he said.

"Not this time," I said with tears in my eyes. "I think I'm going to lose my best girl—she dying."

I turned and raced up the hospital steps, the vendor follow me. Taking my arm, he said, "No, you won't lose her. I'll go with you and we'll pray to God. I'll give her this bunch of roses. They're for life and health. Come on, lead me to her room and we'll pray to Jesus Christ together."

The elevator was waiting when we got to it. I pushed the button for the seventh floor. When the elevator door opened on her floor, I saw the doctor and the nurse in the hall outside Marge's room.

I knew by the look on their faces that Marge was gone.

"I'm sorry," the doctor said. "Your wife has just died. Do you want to go in and see her?"

"Oh my god, we're too late," I heard the flower vendor say.

"You mean," I said, "Marge is gone.... She's not here.... Gone. She's really gone," I said with tears running done my face.

"Yes, she's gone," the doctor said sadly. "Do you want to see her?"

"You say she's gone and you want to know if I want to see her. No—I already saw her with all those tubes and machines around her. No! I don't want to see her if she's gone. Just leave me alone."

XV

THE PHILOSOPHER

> *The idea of philosophy is truth; the idea of religion is life.*
>
> *Peter Bayne 1830-96*

When I went into the funeral parlor to see Marge for the first time since the hospital, I didn't know what to expect. I had told my brother Al, to take care of all the arrangements, and my mother took care of the children. When I saw Marge lay out in her casket, she took my breath away. She was so beautiful. She looked as beautiful as the first day I had met her. She looked as if she were sleeping like the sleeping beauty in the fairy story. I felt that I could go up to her and kiss her and she would wake up. They had made her look like the photographs my brother had given them. She had been so thin and pale and now she was back looking like the girl I had married twelve years ago. But, when I touched her, it was like touching a piece of wood. I knew that she wasn't there.

After the funeral, Marge's mother, Lily, said, "Marge will be able to take a lot better care of her family now that she's in heaven. She would never leave her family and not take care them. She'll watch over all of you."

Just nodding my head, I thought to myself, small chance of that ever being true. I did not mean that Marge wouldn't help her husband and family if she could and God knows she's a saint if anybody is, but, like that old Baptist's hymn, *That Old Rugged Cross,* life can sure get rugged. Like that other old Baptist's song, I would rather be *leaning on the Lord, Safe and Secure.*

I wrote a letter to my cousin in Montreal about six weeks after Marge died where I said, "I don't know what my job is anymore. To pay the bills, I can manage. To be a mother to my children seems almost impossible. To find someone who could take their mother's place seems improbable if not impossible. The woman would have to be "tops" and these are few and far between. What are not already married are in a convent. No! I'm afraid, it will never happen. Just tell some woman, "I want you to meet a widower who has seven children." And that woman will turn and run and I wouldn't blame them. Because it's summer time, I am able to hire teenage girls to baby-sit for five dollars a day during the day while I went to work. Come September, these teenagers will be back in school and I will have to hire someone, perhaps to stay all week and be off on weekends. I'll try and get someone for forty dollars a week with room and board."

I found myself living each day with invisible tears in my eyes, incredible pain in my heart, and indelible memories of what I had and had lost. Not a fast lost but a long, hard, painful lost. I find myself feeling sorry for myself and for the children because they now have no mother. "She'll watch over all of you," her mother said. Oh, sure! How?

Depending on Marge now that she is gone or any Saint for help doesn't seem to fit. It's hard to understand what concern or power any saint would have for our intercession with God. Furthermore, most of our prayers are directed to God. Saints are secondary. Why bother with saints if you can talk directly to the boss? Why a middleman? Especially when the boss is so omnipotent, benevolent and understanding. I'm not saying that saints are not made and that they don't have a special place with God. This may be, but I think that the title is a degree of honor mostly. Who knows what influence they have after death?

The few saints that the Catholic Church has proclaimed are not even the tip of the iceberg. There must be millions and millions of saints in heaven if you define saints as being associated with God. Yet many pray to saints and I don't think there's anything wrong with that. God knows us and understands us better then we understand Him. So, he gets the message anyway.

Luckily, God chooses to understand us even if we don't understand Him. So, I believe there are millions of saints who the Church have never proclaimed and who never had a religious vocation in the Church.

My idea of a saint is a person who lives by the Golden Rule and does his duty to his fellow man and keeps the philosophy of the Ten Commandments in his everyday life. It's a person who can do his job to the best of his ability and then some. A person does his best and a little extra. It's that little bit extra, unselfish effort for others that gain sainthood in the eyes of God, I think.

That's why mothers are mostly saints. Can you think of anyone who has more unselfish love then a mother for her child? And they are consistent … always faithful and true. As Caesar said, "I am as constant as the Northern Star."

Christ was more than a saint, but he didn't spend all his time in the temple praying. No, he was out among the people of all walks of life, helping them, loving them, and teaching them to love one another.

Trying to understand death after a traumatic loss leads one to religion and God. Hungry for the right words, I turned to books. What did the great thinkers of our world have to say about death? Augustine, Aquinas and Luther were too academic for my needs. Descartes was interesting with his *"I think, therefore I am"* thesis. And Nietzsche left me cold with his *superman*. Plato came the closest to the truth that I was seeking. And Christ and the Bible, I suspect, is the truth.

Searching the Bible and reading the Dialogues of Plato, I did find some consolation. Both Christ and Socrates had a lot to say about death and they both faced an untimely death. Each had time to think about their inevitable demise.

Christ said, "Father, if it be your will, remove this cup." Christ knew that after Good Friday, there would be His Easter Sunday with all of its glory. Yet given his choice as a human, he would rather have stayed with his job of teaching and helping people and avoid this death on the cross. But God has some plans that are not easily understood by humans and take priority to our will. So, "Thy will be done." Christ said.

As the Son of God, Christ knew that this was the best way. *Anyone who does the will of my Father will never die. And, though he is dead, he will live.* Strange words the assertion that God knows what he's doing, began to make some sense to me. I have to admit that if God is omnipotent, then He must be a lot smarter than I am. So be it. It behooves me to go along with Him, even when I don't understand what He's doing.

Then sometimes, I think that when things go wrong, it's not really God's will in the true sense of the word. God has willed that there be a certain cause and effect in nature. If we jump off a bridge, well, we just have to suffer the consequences. God is not likely to perform a miracle to save some dummy that won't use his head. God gave us brains, He expects us to use them. And if we're going to be stupid about it, then cause and effect is still God's law.

Socrates said, "Life is a journey from the mortal towards the divine." Socrates believed that a philosopher spends his life preparing for death. He said, "we should keep ourselves pure until the hour when God himself is pleased to release us from this life." This statement eliminates suicide and genocide as a solution to our problems. Socrates said that the oracle [God] that had directed him throughout all his life did not oppose this last judgment of death the citizens of Athens had given him.

So, therefore, the end result must be good. *And those of us who think that death is an evil are in error.* It was as if Socrates was reading the 23rd Psalm *though I shall walk through the valley of death, I shall not fear,* when Socrates said, … *know of a certainty, that no evil can happen to a good man, either in life or after death.* His dialogue anticipates the Christian philosophy when he states, *we ought not to retaliate or render evil for evil to anyone.* Christians use the *Golden Rule.*

It is interesting to note that Socrates did not fear death. "The fear of death," he said, "is indeed the pretense of knowledge and not real wisdom. No one knows that this death they fear as the greatest evil may be but the greatest good. A man who is good for anything," Socrates stated, "ought not to calculate the chance of living or dying; he ought only to consider whether in doing anything, he is doing right or wrong, acting the part of a good man or a bad man."

Socrates further said, "the unexamined life is not worth living … the difficulty my friend, is not to avoid death, but to avoid unrighteousness; for that runs faster then death."

Billy Graham, the evangelist, was quoted as saying when speaking of death, … if we live with God, we will live until God calls us and we die, and then we will live forever with God.

It appears that the best argument for religion and God is death. If there is a life after death, then it behooves us to live in such a way as to warranty a good eternity after death. Life is short and eternity is a long, a very long time.

The riddle of life: Why are we here? Where are we going? And what will we do when we get there? The meditation on these questions leads one to theology for a logical explanation. I was compelled to acknowledge an existence of some supreme power. Call that power God, or what ever you will. Also, because death is so final, it staggers the mind. There is no debate after the event. There is no chance to reconsider. You can't take it to a higher court to reverse the decision. Death is a total and final cut-off of all communications, and I suspect that there is an end to the decision making process of our being.

That is the shocking part of death: It is so abrupt and conclusive. We try to avoid the contemplation of death. We feel that if we ignore it, it will go away and it won't happen to us. But even if we ignore death until God calls us, eventually the aging of our bodies will force us to consider it. It's interesting to note that in this final hour, some who live until God calls them and they *shed this mortal coil* will die and then live forever.

Still, the lost of a love one is difficult for the survivor. We are all part of mankind, as John Donne must have known when he wrote that when a person dies, part of us dies. Since we are all part of humanity, part of our humanity also dies. Many of us feel the lost more than others. It becomes more personal. We cry for our loss love and ourselves. We tend to abandon the future. *No man is an island.... So, don't ask, "For whom the bell tolls ... it tolls for thee.*—John Donne 1573-1631.

And life goes on. In spite of our skepticism and doubt, we try to look forward to the future. It has been said that yesterday is a dream and tomorrow is a hope and today is a gift and that's why we call it the present. Every day on earth is a gift from God. So today, we can plan for the future. We hope there will be events that will lift us out of our gloom and lift us to new heights if we only believe—the sun will shine tomorrow. *Do you believe?*

Bishop Sheen once wrote a book titled *Life Is Worth Living*. He said that happiness in this life was part of God's plan for every one of us. Happiness the likes of which we could never have dreamed or wildly anticipated with our minute intelligence, if only we could believe. Christ was right when he said, *Oh, ye of little faith!*

I wonder about some definitions: Socrates said that a philosopher is a seeker of the truth. Isn't every one of us a philosopher? A Ph.D. or Doctor of Philosophy is one who has made a contribution to the truth. Shouldn't Christ and Socrates be given a Ph.D.?

Of course! But the paper attesting to a degree is not important. It's what you have done for someone else that's important.

Parenthood is a gift from God that forces us to think of somebody else instead of ourselves bringing joy to our lives. Parents are important, especially mothers. Their unselfish love gives them the perfect opportunity to do something for somebody else without any expectations of getting something back. That's what this whole world is about—an opportunity to do something for somebody else. So I think that we can stop feeling sorry for ourselves if we can do something for somebody else—quick. And it is best if that somebody never finds out who did it. God knows—I'm trying!

BOOK II

ONE PLUS ONE EQUALS NINETEEN

*This book is dedicated to Delores, my loving wife of thirty three years, and to our seventeen children, who made our **joint venture** such a happy and wonderful journey by giving us all their unselfish love and devotional support through out the years.*

PREFACE

What's in a Title? *What rationale would persuade a single man with seven children and a single woman with ten children to marry and have a family of nineteen?*

To examine this query, I originally planned this work to be in two phases, that is, two books. Book One would be the story of my original family with seven children, and book two would be the story of the added eleven dependents. The title would be *Seven Come Eleven*. I planned book one to shed some light on my early environmental background … my single years and my first marriage experiences that had conditioned me to take on this new responsibility with any hope for success. It would narrate a lot of my thinking up to the time I was left with my seven small children after my wife died.

Book II would relate the many problems and their solutions that we encountered with a family of nineteen and our many attempts to teach the children the difference between right and wrong, and our "preachings" for their edification and guidance. We felt they would have a better chance in life if we did our job well.

After friends critiqued my first drafts, they said it was like a song with highs and lows melting in with the symphony of life. They encouraged me to publish this manuscript. Later, when rewriting my manuscript, I was fortunate to obtain some astute counseling from a former Holy Redeemer School acquaintance, the renowned mystery writer William X. Kienzle, who had written at that time more than twenty mystery novels, including the *Rosary Murders* which was made into a movie of the same name. Bill's wife, Javan, a retired proofreader and editor from the Detroit Free Press, reviewed my manuscript and made many corrections.

After talking with Bill and Javan, I again changed the title to simply *Seventeen* and book's one and two were combined into one manuscript. Having been rejected by several publishers and at Bill Kienzle's suggestion, I solicited Berl Falbaum, an author and professional public-relations specialist, former reporter for The Detroit News, and teacher at two state universities, to assist me in the final rewrite version of my manuscript for self-publication. I then continued my effort to combine the two parts into one book and returned to the title "*Seven Come Eleven.*" But after many discussions with Berl and his suggestion that I focus on "seventeen," it became clear to me that because of the total distinction and uniqueness of the two parts, I really had two stories that could not be told together as one book. The "Book I part is much like a Shakespearean tragedy that tells the story of how fate, with the *slings and arrows of outrageous fortune*, had dealt an average man a devastating blow destroying his "blue heaven."

Book II is a lighthearted comedy that tells the story of how one widow and one widower merged in a joint venture of marriage to raise seventeen children. "Book one," the tragedy, was abandoned for now. And, at the suggestion of Berl, my astute critic and proofreader, the final result and title of my Book II is now called *One Plus One Equals Nineteen.* Thus, I hope *One Plus One Equals Nineteen* answers for readers the question why Delores and I formed a union to raise seventeen children. More important, we hope readers will learn of the immense joy and love we have experienced through out the years.

ACKNOWLEDGEMENTS

Delores A. Arsenault: Graduate of Marygrove College with a Bachelor's Degree in Early Education, teacher, mother, and my dear wife and constant companion. Thank you for your love, wit, wisdom, and your unfailing support for thirty-four years. You have been my faithful partner giving me strength and guidance during all these many years. "*You're right from heaven ... oh, I know your worth. You've made a heaven ... for me ... right here ... on earth.*"

Seventeen Arsenault/McMillan Children: You know who you are. Thank you for being the best, the brightest, and the kindest, most considerate children in the world and making your mother and me the proudest parents in the world.

The Dominican Sisters: We are especially indebted to the Dominican Sisters who taught our large family when we were just starting our marriage. In the first year of our marriage, they accepted six young Arsenaults at St. Clare of Montefalco School, making a total start of ten Arsenault/McMillan's in their school. Their total enthusiastic encouragement, prayers, and kind consideration, will always be part of our gratitude.

Friends and Relations: A special thanks goes to all our friends and relations who have been our encouragement and faithful supporters in this challenging experience from the very beginning. It was with their good wishes and prayers that helped us succeed.

I

STRANGERS

> *Every heart has its secret sorrows, which the world knows not,*
> *And oftentimes we call a man cold when he is only sad.*
>
> Longfellow 1807-1882

My wife, Marge, died of a brain tumor in May 1964, and I found myself a single man with seven children, trying to avoid the reality of my sorrows. I became cold in my empathy for others. I lost the joy of living each day. I just wanted to get away … go away. I was a stranger in a world where life had no future for me. I knew that I was grieving and I had concern for the children's loss as well and so, a few weeks later, I decided to take the six oldest children on a two-week vacation to visit my uncles, aunts, and cousins in Quebec, Canada. My two-year-old baby, Janet, stayed with my widowed mother, who had taken care of her the past year while Marge was in and out of the hospital. Taking this vacation to Gaspe', Canada helped take my mind off myself, but when we returned from this vacation, I was still miserable.

How can you have a house full of kids and still be alone? Analogy: lost in the middle of the ocean on a raft … water, water everywhere and not a drop to drink. A single parent having a large family is not the best situation. Now, without my wife, I had to make all the family decisions alone.

As I adjusted to this new single-parent life, Saturday night became my night to go out and find distractions. As my brother said, "Do something ... visit somebody." So, on Fridays, after work, I would pick up my mother and baby Janet and bring them to my house in Allen Park. She would stay every weekend with the children. On Sunday, after church, I would return my mother and Janet to my mother's house. During the week, I had numerous housekeepers, nannies, and baby-sitters. But, on the weekends, my mother provided a means for me to seek some diversions and distractions in my sorrow.

But visiting old friends, alone, didn't work out too well. I could tell that they were uncomfortable, and so was I. What do you talk about? My problems were not theirs. We had nothing in common anymore. My loneliness seemed to thunder out at me in my mind as I struggled to find a subject to talk about. Finding and making new friends is easier said than done.

I went to the Thunderbowl Lanes bowling alley near my home in Allen Park and I was told that a mixed league on Sunday afternoon needed bowlers. So, I signed up to bowl with a group of single people who were in there twenties. They were about ten years younger than me. However, this diversion helped to wile away the time ... take my mind off my problems. The bowlers were all very nice ... but I still felt somewhat out of place.

During the following summer ... in 1965, my brother, Al, tried to help me by suggesting that I join some clubs, and meet new people. I didn't feel much like doing either. I was still melancholy and filled with self-pity. But Al persisted. He had read in the local papers about a group at the YMCA called *Parents Without Partners*, and another group, that he had read about in the Michigan Catholic newspaper called *The Naim Conference* which consists of only Catholic widows and widowers. "And it's not all old people," he said "I read that they have an age limit of fifty-five. These clubs are for guys like you. They have dances and other diversions like picnics for the children. You might enjoy their activities."

"Thanks, but I'm not in the mood."

"You should give it a try," he persisted, ignoring my protests. "Go to one of their meetings."

"Okay, okay," I relented. "I'll give it a try. But don't worry about me so much. I'll get by."

Parents Without Partners

The first meeting I attended was that of Parents Without Partners in nearby Lincoln Park because of the proximity to my home. Almost all the women and men I met were divorced. I also discovered that the ratio between the women and men was about six women to every man. Most were about my age and with children. They all were congenial and polite and I felt comfortable talking to them, because we all had similar problems raising children without spouses. During the next few months, I met many single parents who said to me, "It's good to get away and talk with adults for a change." Also, when the children are small, there is a need to evaluate issues, problems, and decisions with an adult. Independent decision-making is not the most desirable method. Joint or group decision-making increases the number of decisions that are correct.

I felt sorry for the divorced mothers because they really had it tougher financially. They had to raise the kids with little support from the fathers. They had to provide for themselves, so that most had to find work, usually starting at the bottom of the wage ladder. Many had little or no credit and drove old cars that always needed repairs, while their former husbands were living like bachelors, working their usual jobs without worrying about the kids. Free as birds, they could run around to bars, go fishing or hunting on weekends, or whatever, without a worry in the world and many times they were late with their child-support payments.

Naim Conference

The night I went downtown to attend my first Naim Conference meeting, I again realized that I was not the only one who had lost a partner to death. A widower named Pat Lynch met me at the door. He introduced himself and I gave him my name. He asked me what parish I was from and how long I was a widower.

The usual inquiry, I thought. "I'm a member of St. Mary Magdalen parish and I live in Allen Park. I've been a widower for over a year."

He asked me how many children I had, and I told him seven.

"I want you to meet a widow that has ten children, and she's about your age."

"Ten! Where does she keep them all?"

He introduced me to Delores. Delores said she lived on the *east side* of Detroit in Grosse Pointe Park. I told her I was from the *west side*. She told me that she had lost her husband of fourteen years to a sudden heart attack three years earlier … in 1962. She said she had heard a thud noise upstairs, as if something heavy had fallen. When she went upstairs, she found him lying on the floor. She called for help but it was too late. He had died of a sudden, unexpected, massive heart attack. She said that she was three months pregnant with her tenth child, and her oldest, Donald, was in the eight grade. Talk about *the going getting tough* … I reflected again that I wasn't the only one that fate had given a bad deal.

Everyone in the Naim group had their own sad story, since they were all widows and widowers. I was introduced to many people, and one young widow, Helen Johnson, lived just a few blocks from me in Allen Park. She too was another widow who had lost her husband to a heart attack, although he had been under a doctor's care for many months before he died. She had a couple of daughters who went to school with some of my children. She said she met my son Patrick while she was a part-time teacher at St. Mary Magdalen grade school. She said that many times Pat looked like he was not paying attention, but when she would question him, he always had all the right answers.

Delores was the activities chairperson. She announced that there was a dance coming next Saturday evening. "Don't miss the Saturday night dance!" she said to all, when giving her report. Helen Johnson came over to me and asked if I was going to the Saturday night dance. I said I would like that and because we lived near each other, why don't I pick her up and save one car. She agreed and I said I would pick her up at seven o'clock sharp.

Dinner Dance

The night of the dinner dance was a balmy summer evening and a good-size crowd was there. The music was great and everyone that could dance was dancing. Helen, whom I had driven to the dance, was dancing with someone and, not being much of a dancer, I was sitting at a table watching. Suddenly, from across the room, I saw an arm waving at me. It was Delores. She was waving at me to come and dance. I went to the dance floor where this "five foot-two, eyes of blue" met me. What a dancer. I had taken five lessons from Arthur Murray's when I got out of the army and knew only the basic magic-box-step. I never was a good dancer! Delores, however, was a beautiful dancer. She reminded me of the dance instructors at Arthur Murray's, who made dancing look so easy. We were doing so well that when the music stopped, we kept right on dancing. I could hear Frank Sinatra singing, *"The band had left the stand and we were still dancing, somewhere on a cloud, off in the blue."*

I had started the evening with Helen but this sensational brunette, named Delores, had taken my breath away. A year later Sinatra would be singing his hit song, Strangers *in the Night,* and with Barbara Streisand's hit, *People.* These two songs seemed to say the things that explained this encounter in this enchanted night.

As the party was breaking up and the dancing was over, I asked Delores, "What's your phone number? Maybe I could give you a call some night when all the children are in bed and we could go out for coffee."

She gave me her phone number and that's how *it* all started ... just a couple of people who enjoyed each other's company. It isn't an easy job for any parent who is a widow or a widower without a partner to be the mother and the father to a lot of children. It's hard on the parent and on the children. I know because I was struggling to keep my family together much as my widowed mother had done for my sister, my brother, and me thirty years ago. The compatibility with people in the same circumstances getting together helps each of them do a better job as parents when they have some adult with the same problems to talk to. That's what the Naim Conference club was all about. It was a supportive club group where I met new friends ... friends that were congruous and sympathetic to my situation. It turned out that my brother was right.

II

PEOPLE

I love these little people; and it is not a slight thing, when they, who are so fresh from God, love us.—Charles Dickens—1812-1870

Joining the Naim Conference was a turning point in my life. I met so many nice people who were in my same situation. We were people who needed people. Everyone had a family to worry about and everyone appreciated the mutual esteem and friendship that the club provided. In just a couple of meetings, I had met someone who made me forget my troubles. I just couldn't get her out of my mind.

A few nights after the dance, I called Delores and asked her if she would like to go out for coffee. She said she would and gave me the directions to her house, and I was off for my first of many trips to Delores's home in Grosse Pointe Park.

I noted the coincidence that I lived in Allen Park on Hanfor Street and Delores lived in Grosse Pointe Park on Balfour Street. We both lived in *parks* and both of our street names ended with *four*. Hanfor and Balfour. Interesting!

When I arrived, I found Delores's house to be a large colonial brick home. Makes sense, I thought, her with ten children. Delores answered the door and stated that it didn't take me long to get there. I told her that it was only seventeen minutes of freeway driving.

"You have a nice size house for your large family," I observed as she led me into the front living room.

"It's adequate. One needs a large house for a large family. Isn't that right?"

"Right! It doesn't make sense to bring children into poverty. Does it?"

"Why do you say that?"

"Well, having a family with ten children takes a lot of resources. One needs to have the means to properly house and nurture a large family so they can get a proper start in this crazy world. Don't you agree?"

"Really?"

"Yes, really. Tell me, why is it so quiet around here? Where are all your children?"

"Oh, they're around. Some are downstairs in the game room, and the others are in the den watching television."

"Are they all as nice as you?"

"They're nicer. You'll see when you meet them. I'll call them when you're ready. They're all anxious to meet you."

"I'm ready."

I sat down on the couch while Delores called the children. Suddenly, in they came from what seemed like all directions.

"This is Mr. Arsenault," she said as they entered the room.

They were all very polite and they impressed me as admirable children, much like my own. I couldn't help making some comparisons between her children and mine as she introduced them to me.

"Are these all of them?" I asked.

"No, my two older boys, Doc, sixteen, and Bob, fifteen, are away studying at the Augustinian Seminary in Holland, Michigan."

"Must be smart boys."

"All my children are smart."

"But why do you call your oldest 'Doc'? Does he plan to become a doctor?"

"No, his name is Donald Robert and his father used his initials DR and nicknamed him Doc. The second oldest is named Robert James."

"Sounds like some kind of a tradition starting, Donald Robert, Robert James, the third boy must be named James-something."

"Could have been. But my third-born was named Timothy John. He should have been named James Timothy or James John, but tradition was thrown out and here is fun-loving Timothy John in person."

"Hello, Mr. Arsenault," he said as we shook hands.

"Then came Joseph Patrick," Delores said.

"There's a coincidence. I have a Patrick Joseph."

Joe stepped forward and, shaking my hand, he said, "I'm Joseph McMillan." Then he offered me his hand again. Shaking his hand a second time really made me feel welcome.

"Joe is our Mr. Fix-it around here," Delores said. "Whenever we have anything broken, we just put it on his workbench and Joe fixes it."

"Every family needs a Mr. Fix-it."

After Joe, I met Martin Dennis and Steven Thomas.

"How old are these two handsome boys?"

"Marty is eight and Steve is six years old."

"My two youngest boys are Robert Ernest and Mark Anthony. They're seven and six"

Delores next introduced me to her four girls. "Another coincidence," I said. "I have four girls too."

"This is my youngest," Delores said, "Mary Ann McMillan."

"Just as pretty as your mother. And how old are you, Mary Ann?"

"I'm two," she said with a cute little smile.

"My youngest is Janet Frances and she's also two years old."

Then I met "sweet Sue" ... Susan Jane McMillan ... her five-year-old, who was the same age as my *sweet* Aileen. I then met Ann Louise, a nine-year-old. "And when were you born?" I asked her.

"I was born on October 16, 1955."

"You were born a year and two months to the day of my daughter Margaret Elizabeth," I said. "She is seven years old but you both were born on the sixteenth of the month."

Then I met Delores's oldest daughter, Patricia Marie. "We call her 'Tish' for short," Delores said. "Tish is eleven years old."

"Tish is the same age as my daughter Mary Ann," I said. "I bet she's as big a help to her mother as my Mary Ann is to me."

"She sure is," Delores said. "But all my children are a big help."

The house was as neat as a pin and so were the children. What an organizer this Delores is, I thought. What a homemaker and manager she must be, to be able to run this large family all by herself, and still have time for the to be Activity Chairperson for the Naim Conference take some doing.

"I'm impressed," I said. "It seems like you have everything under control."

"What do you mean 'control'?"

"I mean that you're a very capable mother."

"Well, when necessity calls, one learns fast," Delores said.

"Yes, you're right, necessity is the mother of invention," I said, quoting an axiom.

"No you don't. You're not pinning that on me," Delores said.

"Oh, you're not the mother of an inventor," I said as we both laughed.

Good sense of humor and pretty too, I thought.

We drove to Kapitski's, a restaurant on Mack Avenue, just two blocks from Delores's home. We talked about the weather and how pleasant it was to get out for a nice breath of fresh air and some conversation after a busy day. Delores said that it was fun to be able to chitchat with an adult after a full day of ten children and all that goes with it.

"Here you are," the waitress said, as she placed two cups of coffee before us.

"Thank you, Ann," Delores said, reading the nametag on the waitress.

"Do I know you two?" the waitress asked.

"No. This is our first time here," Delores said. "If you knew us you wouldn't forget us."

"Why is that?"

"Well," Delores said, "you see, I'm a widow and he's a widower and together we have seventeen children and we're engaged to be married."

"I can't believe it," the waitress said. "Hey, Mable," she said turning to another waitress nearby clearing a table. "Do you know how many children this young couple have?"

"No, how many?"

"Seventeen! This nice young couple have seventeen children together and they are engaged to be married. Can you believe that?"

Everyone in the place was now looking at us.

"Well, bless my soul," Mable said. "God bless them."

I couldn't believe my ears. What was Delores saying? This was our first time out and she's telling the waitress we're engaged to be married and that we have seventeen children. "Delores," I said in a whisper, "what are you telling these people?"

"Oh, I just wanted to see the look on their faces."

"Look on their faces? Delores, you surprise me. I never expected a refined person like you to tell the world about the number of children you or we have and then stated that we are engaged to be married. Are you kidding?"

"Of course I'm kidding. What do you mean 'number of children we have'?"

"I mean I never tell people that I'm a widower with seven children, all under twelve years old. It leads to too many questions and I feel that I have to defend my situation. They wouldn't understand."

"Oh, I don't know," she said. "I always tell everyone I know that I have ten beautiful children. I even carry pictures in my purse to show them." Removing a large wallet from her purse, Delores unfolded a whole string of pictures of her children.

Well, I learned something about Delores. She was a woman with a real sense of humor and she was happy and proud of her family. I realized she had a point.

"OK, you're right to be pleased with your family," I said. "But did you have to tell them we were engaged to be married? Really, Delores, you've got the whole restaurant talking about us. Look over there at that table near the door. The waitress is telling them and they're looking right at us. Let's get out of here. They'll be talking about us after we leave."

"Oh, you're just imagining things."

"Delores, let's get out of here before you tell another story."

"George, don't be so serious. It's just for fun."

"Sure, just for fun," I said as I got up and put some money on the table for the bill.

Diamond Ring

A couple days later, we went to another restaurant, a pizza place on Jefferson, not too far from Balfour Road. This time I was prepared for Delores' "announcement" of our engagement. I had gone to a novelty store and bought a big glass "diamond" engagement ring for ten dollars. I went to a jewelry store and bought a beautiful box for the ring for a couple more dollars. As we were sipping our cup of coffee and talking about children, I took out this little box from my pocket and said, "Here's a little something for you." I handed her the little package wrapped with a gold ribbon.

"Oh, George," she said, as she carefully opened the package and revealed the large "diamond" ring with a little note inside the box.

> ### WILL YOU MARRY ME?
> *Love,*
> *C'est moi*
> *George*

"Oh, George … you shouldn't have … and look at the size of this diamond … It's so big. George … no, no … I really couldn't. You really shouldn't have done this. It's too soon, too fast. I need time to think. No, take the ring back and get your money … I can't accept this. I need more time," she said as she handed the box back to me.

"You just take all the time you want," I said refusing to accept it. "You keep the ring no matter what your decision is. It'll be just a token present of our friendship."

"I've never seen one that was self-adjustable before," she said as she took it out of the box and saw the split band. "This must be something new," she said as she began to realize the true value of the ring. "It seems like a good idea, doesn't it?"

"Yes," I said. "That's the way it is when you buy the very best. You get the latest fashion and design."

"You devil! This is a fake ring, isn't it?"

"Now we're even," I said. "After that little engagement party you pulled on me the other night, I thought that you deserved some special gift."

"But … that was just for fun."

"This is just for fun too."

We were just dreaming out loud. At the time, we both knew marriage was a serious commitment not to be taken lightly … but wouldn't it be nice if it were possible?

The conversation turned to the feasibility of two people like us forming a partnership in marriage and raising seventeen children. "What would people say if we told them we were really thinking of getting married and raising seventeen children in one household?" I said. "I shudder to think about it."

"But what can they say? They would probably try to talk us out of it."

"Can you believe that if two people like us were to ever marry … the problems there would be? Think of it, seventeen children and a wife would make me the unique wage earner with nineteen dependents. Wow! The computers at General Motors would close down. Uncle Sam's IRS would never believe us."

"Well, I guess that any taxpayer who suddenly increases his dependents from seven children to seventeen children does seem a little unusual," Delores said.

"No big deal," I said. "Doesn't it happen every day?" We both laughed.

III

WHO'S WHO

> *The family was ordained by God ... the first form of the church on earth.*
>
> William Aikman 1682-1731

When one suddenly meets ten new people, whether they are adults or children, it's not easy to remember their names. Everyone wants to be called by his or her name and that goes for children too. When I first met Delores's children, I thought that nametags would have been a big help to me. But, it became easier to remember who's who after many months getting to know them. However, remembering their birthdays required more effort. I knew that we had a birthday in every month of the year except August. Some months had two birthdays, ... February, April, May, June, and July. We even had one month with four birthdays. March and two of those were on the tenth of March. Seemed easy enough. As to whose birthday was on a given day, we needed to look at the program listing.

Joint Venture

As we met more and more often, we kept talking about our two families, noting the similarities and coincidences, and there were many. During the autumn months that followed, we talked about the future. We seemed to find ourselves very much in love, and marriage was a subject that we had discussed but seemed out of the question. A family of nineteen would demand a lot from everybody. But as time went on and weeks turned to months, a possible marriage, or, as I called it, a merger and joint venture, became a subject we discussed often and more seriously.

Meanwhile, I found that each day was another happy day to talk to Delores. She was great and fun to be with. Her sparkling personality and good humor along with her good common sense captivated me. As the song said, *I'm just like putty in the hands of a girl like you.* I was crazy about *the kisses of Delores.*

I wrote Delores a letter telling her how much I loved her. Delores liked my letter and told me to keep writing. So I spent many a night writing Delores, telling her how much she meant to me and telling her how she had turned my life around and let me *walk in the sun once more.* Delores would write me notes and sign them *ME.* Now here was another coincidence. My wife, Margaret Elizabeth, left me notes signed *ME.* So, I when I left her notes, I signed my name as *ME* but in French: *c'est moi*, meaning *it's* me, or *it's I.*

We went to see many stage shows in the area. The songs in *Camelot; C'est Moi* and *If Ever I Would Leave You,* fitted right in with our romance. We saw *My Fair Lady* and *I've Grown Accustomed to Her Face* and I *Could Have Danced All Night* seemed to have been written just for us.

Everything seemed to point to our love for each other and the eventuality of our marriage and the merging of our two families into a seemingly impossible joint venture began to become more and more plausible.

"Delores, I have a present for you. It's a copy of *Who Gets the Drumstick* by Helen Beardsley. It's the story of a family of eighteen children with a widow and widower as the father and mother. This is the book that the movie *Yours, Mine and Ours* were based on. I thought that it's too much a coincidence to ignore."

"Yes, I read about that movie with Lucille Ball and Henry Fonda. We'll have to see it. I hear that after they were married, they had two more children, thus it was *your* children, *my* children, and *our* children. However, for us it will be only *our* children even if we have another, they will all be *our* children. Agreed?"

"Of course, I agree. It's the writing on the wall, Delores. Heaven is sure trying to tell us something. If we don't get married and make a go of this thing, we're apt to be struck down by a bolt of lightning."

"Well, if it can be done, it'll take a lot of planning and a lot of praying," Delores prudently said.

"The children all seem to get along fine," I submitted,"

And, financially you have as much income as I have, so together we can cut our overhead of maintaining two houses and have only one large house. That should be a big cost savings. General Motors will pay the medical insurance of all of us. There's several hundred dollars of savings per month right there. I'm sure we can do it financially. You've heard of that movie *Cheaper by the Dozen*. Ours will be cheaper by the dozen and a half."

"Maybe if we say a *Novena* together, everything will work out," Delores suggested.

"Sure, I'll say a novena with you. What are the prayers and for how long?"

"It's a Novena booklet with special prayers to our blessed mother and you have to say it every day for twenty seven days of petitions and twenty-seven days of thanksgiving. Will you do it?"

"Why not. I remember reading of some saint that said, *pray as if everything depended on God and work as if everything depended on you.* If that's the key to success, how can I argue?"

"A marriage like ours will not be easy and we know of a few marriages where a widow and widower combining two families of children that ended up in the divorce courts."

"Yes, I know. And they were small families of five and seven. One couple where the wife had one fifteen-year-old boy and the husband had five of his own went on to have another baby together for an *ours,* and they failed."

"But, there was a big flaw," Delores said. "That husband became an alcoholic and that's why they failed."

"Well, we don't have the time nor the money to become alcoholics," I said.

"One Naim Conference widow who married had a nervous breakdown. And remember the mother who had one teenage boy married the widower with five small children? The small children just could not accept the new mother."

"You're right. Some of these marriages should never have happened. It's not easy for sure. The children's agreeing to the union is very important."

"I think all our children appear to be happy together. But, we'll say the Novena anyway, and maybe Heaven will help us. I said a Novena before my first marriage and it turned out all right," Delores said.

"It's all right by me and it can't hurt anything. I'm willing to say the Novena if you are. Just saying these prayers in this small book for fifty four days should do it, right?"

"That's right," Delores explained, "twenty seven days petition and twenty seven days thanksgiving whether you think you got the favor or not. That's the Novena and it only takes about fifteen minutes each day."

"It doesn't make much sense to pray 27 days thanksgiving if you don't get the favor."

"The premise is that you really did get an answer and the answer was '*no!*' That means that it was better for you not to get the favor."

"Meanwhile we'll continue planning," I said. "I'll make up a budget, and we'll start looking for a home big enough for seventeen

children. We can't get married until we find one … that's all there
is to that.

We'll just say it's God's will," Delores added, "and we'll keep going
the way we are now with separate families. One can raise a family
in a small house but one cannot start with a big family unless one
has a suitable house for them. Don't you agree?"

"Yes! Unless everything works out, the marriage will have to
wait. However, when we do find the right house, we can start our
joint venture. We're like two companies who join forces to achieve
an objective. I'll put it in writing and send you *An Analysis of Unity*
hypothesis for this joint ventured in my next letter."

The following is my *Analysis of Unity* hypothesis that I wrote and
sent to Delores with the hope of convincing her that this marriage
was both economically feasible as well as socially acceptable. I tried
to plan this union, as a businessman would devise a business plan.

Analysis of Unity

What benefits can we expect by uniting these two separate *companies* into a single joint venture operating as one entity? Along
with the happiness of nineteen people, we could cite the economics
of scale cost savings. The saving benefits of thrifty buying in larger
quantities along with the savings realized from other joint planning will be our goal.

For example, since our separate families were subsisting and man-
aging as separate and independent families, we could expect financial savings right from the start by combining resources and efforts.
By using one home for both families, we could expect to immediately
save on utilities, property taxes and home insurance. The cost of GM's
MIC General auto insurance provided approximately a twenty percent
discount on the cost of collision, comprehensive coverage, property
damage, bodily injury, personal injury insurance costs when a second

car was part of the insurance package. This was a substantial savings for auto insurance. We could expect to reduce our overhead costs for taxes, gas, electric, water and telephones costs between Allen Park and Grosse Pointe Park and show considerable savings. By careful planning, we could expect to reduce the cost of many other items, using large-scale purchasing power and discounts.

By careful planning and organizing, we can also expect to create efficiency in the duties and chores required for a first class family. The proper use of the available manpower (nine boys and eight girls) would lighten the tasks around the house and with fewer burdens for everyone and produce the best good housekeeping standards with a minimum of effort by everyone. The increased efficiency along with the interchange of vital data of past experiences between and with the added advantage of many heads *brain storming* for the common goal, should produce a decided reduction of the load and burden on top management (you and I) thus providing an increase of the happiness and joy for all the members of this new joint company (family).

The development of this thesis as we continue should result in more benefits for this joint venture. With careful examination and testing, these savings and efficiencies could be expected to continue as new ideas and methods are developed from time to time, contributing to the ease and comfort of all members of the company. It was more than probable that every one of us could increase our efficiency more than fifty percent, thus increasing our happiness and joy more than one hundred percent.

The primary and most valuable reason of uniting our mutual love is for the total consideration of others. The love of two individuals that emphasizes the unselfish consideration for others (the children) is a powerful force, which can bring the joy of great accomplishment within our reach as well as provide the children in the family the happiness of growing up with loving parents and brothers and sisters. Our objective will be to raise our girls to be perfect ladies and our boys to be perfect gentlemen.

The communication with those we love and the example of our love can provide the essential ingredients for individual personal happiness as well as the salvation of their very souls. We must face the facts and not fail to realize the benefits of this association for the good of all. If I were God, and I had two people, ... a man and a woman ... who were willing to be the father and mother to seventeen very valuable children, I would make it easy for them to make this happen. The fears, worries, and anxieties that may stem from this proposal can be dealt with adequately and successfully with the proper planning, organizing and control by the managers.

Love can produce poise, satisfaction, self-confidence and bountiful energy in all members of the family. With our trust in God and His unselfish love, we could create a beautiful symphony for God. These seventeen children may someday be the elements that can contribute to the greatness of God in the world. This was not a matter of chance but a positive trust in God that would help us to succeed in our venture.

Look at the fun we would have proving that unselfish love can conquer all obstacles making this joint venture a success. If we could manage to be wise enough to learn the right things and avoid learning the wrong things, then success would be guaranteed. It would be a challenge devoutly to be desired. The greatest treasure of life which cannot be corrupted and which we can take with us into the next world is pure love ... true unselfish love ... a divine reflection of God Himself. And remember, with God, all things are possible.

Step Parents

So, a joint venture of marriage and the combining of our families of seventeen children were agreed upon providing we felt we could solve the problems that would come with this alliance. Will this marriage last? Can two people raise seventeen children and do a good job? Can the different personalities in children cause incompatibility? Will the children accept the stepparent? How do you raise seventeen children and have them grow up as good loving people who are honest, kind, considerate, ambitious and hard working citizens of this great country? These were some of the questions that people asked when we first talked about the impending marriage. I think that it all depends on what the similarities and the differences are in the parents. Some differences are good since *opposites attract* and *variety is the spice of life*. But unity and unity of purpose, and setting good examples by the parents, is the common bond. Respect for each individual child as a unique gift from God was also part of our common bond.

"Can it succeed?" We were not sure when we first started. It took the solving of each problem on a day-to-day basis in order to make a venture like this work. Everyone in the family knew that this was necessary. They all knew that everyone would have to help to make it a success. But they knew that it was a worthwhile venture that would reap tons of rewards. They knew that they could be better than they were.

Delores and I knew that it would not be an easy task. There were many problems, the most immediate being the sale of both our homes and finding one big enough to accommodate the new family. How much money would we need and how large a mortgage could we afford to take on? The house would have to have six or more bedrooms with baths and that's a big house. Finding the right house would have to be our first objective before we would put our houses up for sale.

Although finding the house and creating feasibility were major challenges, these issues gave me a chance to apply my thesis of scientific decision-making. When studying management at the Detroit College of Business in Dearborn, Michigan, I developed the following thesis if I were ever to pursue a doctorate's degree:

1. Identify the problem.
2. Collect data.
3. Analyze and hypothesize.
4. Testing.
5. Application and review.

Thus, we had to identify the problem or problems that would be confronting our marriage. How do we identify the problem? Ask questions. What kind of questions? Questions pertinent to the problem. The more pertinent is the question, the easier it is to identify the problem. Once we identified the problem, then we collected data. What kind of data? Well, of course, data pertinent to the problem.

One of the first question we faced was: How will the ten McMillan children get along with the seven Arsenault children? The data pertinent to this question could be collected at a family picnic with all the children. Together, Delores and I could carefully observe how the children got along. The date for the picnic was set and our two nine passenger station wagons were adequate to transport these seventeen children to the Huron Valley Park. Delores' two older boys were home from the seminary and were a great help with the smaller children. Even though Doc and Bob were fifteen and sixteen years old, they were excited about the picnic and were happy to attend. They were the goodwill ambassadors who acted as counselors and really showed their leadership abilities. I was quite surprised and delighted. This was the beginning of our scientific analysis.

The two station wagons with two adults and seventeen children converged on Huron River Park early on a Saturday morning in April. The weather was perfect for this special picnic where two anxious parents without partners watched carefully as the children were introduced to each other.

Since six of my children were the same age as six of Delores' children, and they seemed to pair up with their new friends, we could see that all was going well. Delores' four older boys were enjoying the games with all the younger children. Once again I recalled that old line from *Cheaper by the Dozen,* and I asked Delores "are these all our children or is this a picnic?"

She remembered the line as well and said, "Yes, these are all <u>our</u> children and believe me, *it's no picnic.*"

We both laughed. But it really was a picnic and they really were our *fun* children.

Managers

It has been said that Americans are the best managers in the world and if three Americans ever got stranded on a desert island, they would immediately form a corporation ... elect a president, secretary and treasurer. Then, they would call for a board meeting to discuss the problems. So it was with us. After the picnic, we had our board meeting and Delores and I discussed the results of the picnic under "old business." The analysis of the question of seventeen children getting along together was a tremendous success. In fact, they seemed to be very happy to have found new friends. Of course, this was only the first question tested. The question now was "would the harmony last?" We would need more ... a lot more ... observations and tests of the relationship between the children.

The next question asked under "new business" was: Where do we put seventeen children? I had a three-bedroom ranch home plus two more bedrooms with a bathroom in the finished basement for my three boys. This was a full house for seven children with parents. Delores had a colonial two-story home with four bedrooms and a large finished third-floor bedroom with a full bathroom and shower for her four older boys.A full house for a family of ten children and parents. Neither home would accommodate a family of nineteen. We would need to either expand one house by adding a couple more bedrooms and baths or buy a house that would already have enough bedrooms and baths. Delores' home was the only one that could be expanded.

Analysis: If we allocate two children per bedroom, we would need eight bedrooms for the children (one bedroom would have three children) and the ninth bedroom for the parents. Also, with nine bedrooms, we would need more than two bathrooms, perhaps even four or five bathrooms. The analysis of this data indicated that we needed to examine whether we could expand Delores' house or buy a new bigger house.

To test the hypothesis of expanding Delores' house, we had an architect draw up plans for a two-floor expansion attachment to the back of Delores' house. Her house was on a large lot that would accommodate such an addition. She also had a two-car unattached garage at the back of the lot to the right of the house that would not interfere with this addition. So for two hundred and fifty dollars, the architect drew up the blue prints and we submitted them to three local builders for cost estimates.

When the estimates came in, we found that the cost would be about the same as the value of the existing house, thus doubling the value of the house. We considered this to be too much money. That left us with the option to buy or build a new house. However, we still had the question: how much can we afford? Analysis: my house in Allen Park had a full mortgage. I had bought it under the *GI bill* with no money down. I had added a garage and some improvements but my estimated value would just pay off the mortgage and not leave much in addition. The real-estate market was, and had been, at a standstill for the past ten years. Delores' house had been paid off with her husband's insurance after his death, so we could put the full value of Delores' house as a down payment on a bigger home and our combined income would allow us to pick up the same amount as a mortgage, thus having doubled the value and size of Delores' house. This we could afford.

Then we asked: where are there large homes that have as many bedrooms and baths that we would need? Grosse Pointe Park had many large homes that would be adequate. Another place was *Grosse Ile*, the little island community about forty miles south of Detroit where the Detroit River empties into Lake Erie. We began checking for homes in Grosse Pointe Park and Grosse Ile for the size home we would need and for the price we could afford.

As we continued, we again realized that our marriage plan was not a simple decision and many questions still needed answering before we could make the move. We knew that *the house* was the biggest hurdle that we had to jump over. Love or no love, the order of business was now to find the *right* house before we could be married. Delores' *Novena* meant praying for the whole scheme, improbable, as it may have seemed. At times, we thought we would need a miracle. They say that 'love will find a way and pray for it.' And we did. We felt that the best marriages are *'made in heaven.'* The way things were going we wondered whether heaven was on our side. Well, the first sign of support from heaven would be ... *the right house.*

IV

FATE OR DESTINY

> *A strict belief in fate is the worst kind of slavery; on the other hand there is comfort in the thought that God will be moved by our prayers.*—*Epicurus 342-270 BC*

"I want some of my friends to meet you," Delores said with a twinkle in her eye. "I've been telling them about you for the last six months and so I'm planning a get together this week end. They're all anxious to meet you."

"Well, isn't that nice," I said. But I thought ... I'd bet they're eager to meet me. They want to meet this guy who has seven kids and is willing to take on ten more children. Must be some kind of a nut. I could hear them now with their wise cracks like an old joke I remembered: "Do you know why God gives children to young people?"

"Because they don't know any better."

I anticipated their thoughts: "Here's a guy who doesn't know any better. Here's a guy, widowed, pushing forty, with seven children, engaged to a widow with ten children. I wonder what's wrong with his thinking?" I could hear them, "Why is he doing this?"

"It's an opportunity few men have!" I would answer.

"It's an opportunity few men want!" they would say.

"All it takes is good management," I would tell them.

"All it takes is dumb courage and blind faith," they would kindly reply.

"Wait a minute," I would counter, "put yourself in my place."

"Not on your life," they would say.

"Now wait," I would persist. "Let's be realistic and face the facts. Suppose you were left alone with seven or ten children ... talk about Parents Without Partners. Don't you think that the job of raising all these children and providing for their needs in growing up would be easier for two experienced adults, ... experienced working together, to manage than for each to be doing this parenting task alone? Consider two veterans, like Delores and myself: Don't you think that we, working together, could and would do a better job than if we had to do it alone? And besides, don't forget love. It takes a lot of love to raise a family and make a home for them. Delores and I love each other very much and we love our children. That should be worth something. By God, I know we can do it with God's help."

"You two had better learn how to pray a lot," they would say, "because you'll need a lot of God's help to make this work."

"But," I would say, "With God's help, we'll concede, all things are possible!"

"I'm afraid that you may need more than God's help and prayer."

"Sure, but remember, we're not just out of school you know. We're veterans in this parenting business, and if anyone can do it, we can."

Touché!

Tea For Two

Seventeen.... what's so special about seventeen? Of course, if seventeen happens to be the number of your dependent children, well, that number takes on a whole new dimension.

Before I was married to Marge, I use to think that two children would be a good number for a family. Like the song, *Tea for Two,* "… a boy for you and a girl for me"

Would be good. However, fate and time have a way of changing ideas. The Catholic Church stated that the main purpose of marriage was to procreate children. Well, that seemed all right with us as long as we were able to financially take care of these children. It's nice to believe that God knows what He's doing and He's in control and that it will all work out for the better. At least, I'd like to think that it would. But, at the age of thirty-nine, I found myself with seven children and soon to have seventeen. Over night, I would be adding eleven more dependents. Seemed hard to believe … father of seventeen children with the youngest three and the oldest, seventeen. If I were to be the father of seventeen children, then it behooves me to be the very best father that I can possibly be. All I had to do was to define *best* and pursue that course. However, *it's easier said than done* as the old saying so aptly puts it.

What occurrences in my upbringing, my youth, could have conditioned me and led me to this event? Did God or fate have anything to do with it? It's not probably. We make our own troubles. However, I believe that God is there to offer help along the way in all circumstances of our own making. What in my past could have conditioned me and prepared me for this stage of my life that I would contemplate and accept the obligation of being the father of seventeen children with some hope for success?

Nine Sons—1966

Front Row: Mark Anthony Arsenault, Steven Thomas McMillan, Martin Dennis McMillan, Robert Ernest Arsenault

Back Row: Joseph Patrick McMillan, Timothy John McMillan, Robert James McMillan, Donald Robert McMillan, Patrick Joseph Arsenault

Eight Daughters—1966

Left to Right: Margaret Elizabeth Arsenault, Ann Louis McMillan, Susan Jane McMillan, Janet Frances Arsenault, Mary Ann Arsenault, Mary Ann McMillan, Patricia Marie McMillan, Aileen Therese Arsenault

V

LA MAISON

> *Houses are built to live in more than to look at; therefore, let use be preferred to uniformity, except where both may be had.*
>
> -F. Bacon 1561-1625.

Getting married is not a simple matter when you have seventeen children of ages three to seventeen to contend with and you must assure for their welfare. There is not only the question of getting them into a school but because of our upbringing, it would have to be a Catholic school. Of my seven children, my three-year-old was with my mother and six were now attending St. Mary Magdalen's Catholic School in Allen Park. Delores' three-year-old was home and six children were attending St. Clare of Montefalco Parish School, one boy was attending the Augustinian Preparatory School for Boys in Detroit and the two older boys were at the Augustinian Seminary in Holland, Michigan. When we married, we would have fifteen children in school and two at home. That's twelve children in grade school, one in high school and two at the seminary. That's quite a bit to manage.

During the time we were resolving our unanswered issues, I was attending night school two days a week at the Detroit College of Business working to finish the requirements for my four-year

Bachelor of Science degree in management. I was studying management decision-making and I tried to apply what I was studying to the issues we faced. I developed a thesis to solve these questions. It struck me that my personal issues were a lot like business problems. We needed to have a five-year plan and have a working budget or we could lose everything.

"Delores," I said, "finding a suitable house seems to be an impossible task. What if we consider keeping the two houses and, just for our analysis, let's consider this union of our new marriage as a business venture and run it like any business. As an accountant with General Motors, I know how to make a budget so that we will know exactly what kind of money we're talking about, what it will cost and we'll treat this union in marriage just like a business *joint venture*. We will operate just like GM."

"How can we do that?"

"Well, by using *POC,* the functions of management: *Plan, Organize and Control.* First, we will decentralize our operation by locations and we will designate managers for our two locations. We can delegate to our assigned managers the necessary authority and autonomy to operate two separate units, one east of Detroit and the other west of the city where they are already situated. Top management … you and I … will open a home office headquarters in downtown Detroit. We will be half way between the east side and west side … our two units of operations."

"Of course, you're kidding?"

"Sure. But it's fun just to suppose and think about it. Besides, just think of the possibilities: we could set up a controls by closed circuit TV; we could maintain both homes as is without any changes; we can have immediate communication by telephone; we can make daily visits to assure that we're not losing control."

"Sorry, George. I don't think that it will work. The cost of setting up another location would be too much. Secondly, children of all ages need constant supervision and delegating that much management responsibility to the older children is too much for any young person. No, George, you'll have to think of something else."

"Now that you mention it, I know that you're right about the cost factor. I know that when GM makes a move, they usually do it to increase their efficiency and reduce costs. We would be increasing our costs and reducing our efficiency. Yeah, you're right. It wouldn't work but it was fun to contemplate. I can think of three reasons why it wouldn't work: First, the cost would be too high. Secondly, the control would be too slow and difficult. And third, as you stated, the parents need to live with all the children."

Since adding on to Delores' house here in Grosse Pointe Park would be too expensive. We now were sure that purchasing a larger house was a better hypothesis than adding on to an existing house. Houses that are designed originally with six or seven bedrooms are better proportioned and having been built with cheaper labor costs is a better buy economically. The *add-on* hypothesis became a mute question.

One of our friends suggested a different proposal suggesting that we buy a small motel at the outskirts of the city. This was an interesting idea. Everyone would have a private room with a private bath and their own closet. We could have a large family room with kitchen for meals and recreation. The problem with this concept was that there were no reasonably priced small motels available in our price range or at a convenient and desirable location. Also, the overhead cost of heat would be too high and maintenance would be a full-time job. So, we quickly scrapped that idea. We were back to finding an existing large house.

We had considered building a new house, but the costs in subdivisions where new homes were being built was beyond our budget. The monthly mortgage payments we could afford indicated that we needed to look in older neighborhoods where prices were more within our reach.

"There has to be a used large house for sale somewhere that would accommodate our needs and would be within our budget," I said to Delores.

"But, George, I'm still not sure that we can afford the costs of buying a larger house and then maintain all the additional expenses of higher taxes and higher utility expenses."

"I've already made a budget and we're in good shape."

"Yes, I know. But, can we be sure we have anticipated all our costs including mortgage payments, property taxes and dozens of other costs?"

"Remember," I said, "there are many cost savings in our *joint venture*. As far as the other costs, that's where you come in. Check my lists of expenses and make sure I didn't miss something. Identifying all our expenditures is mandatory to our success. Let me put it this way. There are two kinds of costs that we have to consider, the same as General Motors or anyone else on a budget. Those costs are *fixed* and *variable*. The fixed costs are reoccurring costs that do not readily change, like insurance payments, property taxes and mortgage payments. These costs are not easily changed. Now, the variable costs are different. Things like food, clothing, recreation and other like expenditures can be changed easily. These costs we can do something about. We don't need a two or three thousand-dollar vacation every year. That's a variable cost that we can forgo to stay within our income and budget. We don't need to hire painters for our house. We can do the painting ourselves and save the money. That's a variable cost. So, there's a lot of ways we can stay within our budget. We don't need to eat at restaurants. We'll eat at home and save some more money."

"No more vacations on the French Riviera, I guess," Delores said with a laugh.

"Right. Now you have the idea. Budgeting is not easy. And a budget is a dynamic plan. It changes as you go and as you make certain value judgments and expenditure decisions. Another savings will be the wear and tear on my car not to mention the cost of gasoline for me driving every day from the west side to the east side."

"Also," Delores added. "Don't forget that my Social Security as a widow would come to a halt but the Social Security payments for the children will continue until they're out of school. So, that's a plus."

"We can also expect a large savings on income taxes with my putting in nineteen dependents," I added. "Variable costs, such as hamburger, hand-me-downs, and local vacations are already the order of the day."

"That sure sounds like a business. But what does it all mean?"

"It means," I said still trying to be business-like, "that we have a good hypothesis that indicates this merger can financially be feasible where all the costs are controlled and *if*. And here's a big *if* ... if we can find *the house* that will have the necessary rooms and be within our budget for mortgage payments, insurance and property taxes."

"I think that both of our families moving into a new house is the best idea," Delores said. "That way when the question comes up with the children of whose house is this, it's not the Arsenault house or the McMillan house, everyone in the family can say, 'it's *our* house ... my mom and dad just bought it ... we just moved in.'"

"I totally agree," nodding my head in concurrence. At present, we have the *Arsenault house* and the *McMillan house*. That would change to *our house.*"

"Then we agree that this would contribute to our goal of family unity and family *esprit de corps.* The house is not yours *or mine* ... the house is *ours*. Our unity would be enhanced as we all become one family living in *our house* under equal and joint ownership."

So, the search for *la maison* continued through the winter of 1965 and into the spring of 1966. Months went by as we searched the papers every day with no luck. It was our thesis that God gave us all these children and He would prefer that they had both a father and a mother, who loved all of them dearly, and all lived in one home. Therefore, it follows that God will provide the necessary means to do this. After fifty-four days or almost two months of praying and searching, we finished the novena and we were still trying to find *the right house.*

The Family

What a family this will be. Imagine seventeen individual children with their unique personalities ... all precious children ... all living as one family in one house. Just for the record, the following is a list of names and birth dates, in chronological order:

1. Donald Robert McMillan	April 16, 1949
2. Robert James McMillan	June 27, 1950
3. Timothy John McMillan	May 14, 1951
4. Joseph Patrick McMillan	March 23, 1953
5. Mary Ann Arsenault	January 9, 1954
6. Patricia Marie McMillan	March 21, 1954
7. Patrick Joseph Arsenault	June 23, 1955
8. Ann Louise McMillan	October 16, 1955
9. Margaret Elizabeth Arsenault	Dec 16, 1956
10. Martin Dennis McMillan	April 5, 1957
11. Robert Ernest Arsenault	February 14, 1958
12. Mark Anthony Arsenault	March 10, 1959
13. Steven Thomas McMillan	July 3, 1959
14. Susan Jane McMillan	May 13, 1960
15. Aileen Therese Arsenault	July 22, 1960
16. Janet Frances Arsenault	November 8, 1962
17. Mary Ann McMillan	March 10, 1963

Everyone is a special person with a very unique and lovable personality. Everyone has his or her own story to tell. As we have always said, "*we wouldn't trade any one of them for a million dollars.*"

VI

LA CHATEAU

> *For a man's house is his castle.-Sir Edward Coke*
> *1552-1634.*

Daily searching the newspapers for available houses and talking to real estate brokers seemed endless and futile. We spent our weekends driving around collecting data on large houses that were for sale in various communities. One day, when I was looking through the Detroit News classified ads, I came across a house with eight bedrooms. I called Delores to tell her the news.

"Delores, I found a house with eight bedrooms."

"Where?"

"On Grosse Isle."

"That's thirty miles from Detroit," Delores said. "Don't you think that that's a little bit too far from your work at Fisher Body Fleetwood in Detroit?"

"Not really with today's cars and good roads. We have a couple of people at Fleetwood that live on Grosse Isle. The head of the payroll department, Bill Kienzle, lives on Grosse Isle and he thinks it's great to get away from the big city. Another guy, an engineer, John Zamit, lives on the island and he says it's like being on vacation all year with the swimming, fishing, right at their doorstep. They call themselves *The Islanders*."

"Well, I suppose it wouldn't do any harm to go look at it. How much are they asking for it?"

"Right in our ballpark ... around fifty thousand. I'll call the realtor and get some more information and make an appointment to see the house."

Grosse Isle

"This house is perfect for you and your family, Mr. Arsenault," the realtor said. "And it is available for immediate occupancy. The owner is a retired couple that lives in Florida. It has eight bedrooms and four baths on the second floor with a half bath on the first and in the basement. It's beautifully situated with lake frontage and a boat well right on the river leading out to Lake Erie. And the best news is that they will let it go for fifty thousand dollars. They were asking eighty thousand a year ago."

The price was within our planned budget so we made arrangements to see this eight-bedroom home on the waterfront

The Castle

Bright and early on a Saturday morning, I picked up Delores. We had 'ready made-live in' baby sitters so that we could go for a couple of hours. We drove west on the Ford Expressway to the interchange and took the Chrysler Expressway downtown to the I-75 Fisher Expressway ... due South ... Driving downriver to Grosse Isle, we wondered just how *perfect* this house would be.

Arriving at the exit for the North River Bridge, we drove over the bridge onto the island to the Realtor's office. She was waiting at the door and motioned to us to park our car in the driveway. She drove us in her Cadillac and gave us a tour of the island before taking us to the *perfect* house. Almost all the roads were either gravel or dirt.

We drove across many small bridges crossing creeks, streams, and twisting in and out around the island. We drove across a small bridge and followed a dusty dirt road until we came to an old rusty iron gate across a driveway. The realtor stopped to open the gate and as we continued up the driveway, we had our first glimpse of the proposed house. I had the feeling that I had seen this place before … a large foreboding three-story house sitting atop a small mound … but where?

"This place reminds me of some place I've already seen," I whispered to Delores. "Now I remember … all we need is some thunder and lightning. It's Dracula's Castle."

It was big all right. The house was situated on an acre of land surrounded by trees and shrubs. Everything was overgrown and unkempt. All the rooms were very large. I seemed to feel a draft going up the main staircase from the entrance hall with its large fireplace. Plenty of dollars to heat this place, I thought. The ceilings were at least ten feet high. I could just see our heating bills in the winter with the dollars flying out the window. The place needed a lot of repair, both mechanical and structural. The walls in all the rooms needed paint and the cracks needed repair. There were even signs of water leaks in some rooms. "Does the roof leak?" I asked the realtor pointing to the ceiling in the master bedroom.

"Yes, the roof does need repairing. But, I already have a contractors estimate for that repair," she said. "I'll give you a copy when we get back to the office. But this house is a handyman's dream."

We went down to the basement where we found a very large room at the foot of the basement stairway, which was finished with a hard wood floor. It had a door going outside and there was a stairway leading to the back yard. Another door from this 'recreation' basement room led to a hallway with smaller rooms attached. Down at the end of the hallway there was a door leading to the furnace room and the laundry room. I looked at the furnace and it was an old coal burning steam boiler that had been converted to oil. Next to the boiler was a large 200-gallon oil tank.

"It's a great investment to make some money in the future," the realtor suggested.

"I'll bet it is," but not for us I thought. The longer we toured this empty house, the more it supported my first impression that this is not the right house.

The price was so reasonable because the house had not been lived in for more than a year and it was run down and the area was run down.

Thanks, but no thanks. We scratch *Dracula's Castle off our list.*

VII

THE HOUSE

The first indication of domestic happiness is the love of one's home.

Frances D. Montlosier 1755-1838.

In the spring of 1966, we were still looking for a house. The world was still going around the sun. That year, *The Man of La Mancha* was named New York's Drama Critics 'Best Musical' where the song *The Quest* was sweeping Broadway off its feet and Delores and I were still pursuing our *quest* for the *impossible dream.*

One day, while driving down some streets in Grosse Pointe Park looking for new *For Sale* signs, I noticed a large home just off Jefferson Avenue on Devonshire Road. It had overgrown shrubbery around it and a large hedge across the front of the house. In the hedge was a *For Sale* sign. When I arrived at Delores' house on Balfour, I told her about this home and we decided to go take a look at it.

Our first impression was that it would be large enough for our needs. The address was *One Thousand*. "Nice address," I said to Delores. "I like the Mediterranean design with a center entrance. Notice how the sun golden bricks with a *Gothic* style of rounded arches for the doors and windows give the house an air of the

Mediterranean Riviera. It also has a slate roof. That type roof will last a hundred years."

The house also had a grape arbor walkway with roman white pillars supporting large wooden crossbeams over the walkway. The arbor walkway started at a screened-in porch at the side of the house facing the vacant attached lot and ends after about forty feet into a large tiled patio with a picnic table sheltered by large fir trees around it. The adjacent lot was filled with fruit trees and shrubs much like a park. Next to the screened-in porch was a flower conservatory complete with a water fountain and glass skylight dome.

"Delores," I said. "Call the realtor tomorrow and find out what they want for this place and make an appointment for us to see it."

"I'll call in the morning. But, I wonder why we haven't seen the for sale sign before. We've been up and down these streets for more than four months now. Can you imagine that *the* house was only a few blocks from my house on Balfour? It looks like the perfect house for our family, but can we afford their price?"

For Sale Again

"Your timing is perfect," the realtor said, " because the house had been sold but since the buyer's mortgage was not approved, the deal fell through. The house just went back on the market this week. Call this number for an appointment with the owners and the owners son or daughter show you around."

"Can you tell me what the price is that they are asking for the house?" Delores asked.

"I know that they had sold it for eighty thousand dollars, but that included thirty thousand for the vacant lot next to it on the corner. She might sell it without the lot for fifty thousand."

When Delores told me about the house and the price, I said, "Bingo! The pieces are starting to fall in place. Will wonders ever cease?"

Touring The House

Delores made an appointment to see the house for the next evening. The owner's daughter said she would be glad to show us around. That evening, we walked up to the front door at exactly six o'clock. The owner's daughter opened the door and invited us into the house. The front door had a large brass handle and the door was rounded at the top. It was solid wood about three inches thick. The entrance was a small marble floor with an equally heavy oak door on each side of the front door leading to two closets. A second door led out of the entrance hall into the lobby where a large staircase led to the upstairs. The entrance alone was very impressive. The realtor had said that the house has about six thousand square feet with nineteen rooms.

"How many bedrooms are there?" I asked.

"There are seven bedrooms and four bathrooms on the second floor. We have two master bedrooms with tub and stall showers. The largest is the main master bedroom. It has a dust balcony, with French doors, overlooking the back-yard patio and a walk-in dressing room closet. Then off the hallway on the second floor, there's a six-by-eight foot walk-in linen closet and a five-by-eight foot walk-in cedar closet."

Touring the first floor, we found a large kitchen with a butler's pantry and a large breakfast room. We then went into a very large dining room with a fireplace at the far end where a leaded glass door led out to a screened-in porch and patio. We continued into the large living room through a sliding door. The living room had a beautiful stone carved fireplace. At the far end of the living room was another leaded glass door to a small conservatory with a glass dome and a fountain with water squirting into a large gold fish pool. The living room and the dining room also both had leaded glass French doors leading into the main entrance room. Down the hall from the entrance room, we were led into the mahogany book cased library room and further down the hall were a half bathroom and a door leading outside to the driveway.

We went down to see the basement using the beautiful front stairway just off the library that was papered with scenes of Paris. There were four large rooms in the basement. One room was fourteen feet by forty-five feet called the "ballroom" that had a hardwood floor and a fireplace. There was even a small bar room attached to the ballroom. Using the back stairway up to the kitchen, we continued up to the second floor and a stairway to the third floor. On the third floor was a very large room that measured about fifty-six feet long and twenty-five feet wide with a very high ceiling under the roof. In my mind, I imagined it to be finished into two large rooms.

Descending to the second floor, we saw the seven bedrooms with four bathrooms. There was a long hallway with a full bath and two bedrooms. This must have been the servants' quarters with these two bedrooms and their own bathroom at the end of this hallway. At the far end of the hallway was a door. Passing through this door and turning left was another long hallway with the grand front staircase about half way down. At the head of the staircase was the master bedroom. It had its own dressing room with bath and stall shower as we had been told. At the start of the hallway was a second bedroom that had its own private bath and stall shower. Down at the far end were two more bedrooms that shared a bathroom between them with each having its own entrance door from their room. At the end of the main hallway, there was another door leading to another room with large windows facing southeast. Our *tour guide* said that this was called the sunroom. On this floor there was also the large walk-in linen closet and a walk-in cedar closet. At the head of the large winding staircase were two French doors leading to a small room with a kneeling bench and a religious icon. This room was used as a chapel, the daughter told us.

The house had three fireplaces … one in the large living room, one in the large dining room, and one in the ballroom in the basement. The house had a four-car attached garage with electronic operating door openers. The garage was set sideways at the back of the house and could not be seen from the front of the house. There was a door to a large attached screened in porch adjacent to the grape arbor walkway that lead to the patio with a picnic table. The dining room also had two French doors leading directly out into another patio adjacent to the screened in porch.

We spent more then an hour and a half just walking through the house. There were so many things of interest to see, like the conservatory with its fountain and skylight ceiling, the dust porch with its French doors with a view of the park-like back yard and the master bedroom with the adjacent sunroom. The screened in back patio, the butler's pantry with its own sink, and the library with a half bathroom next to it was very appealing. There were seven doors leading to the outside from the first floor. There were even two basement doors leading out to the back yard.

As we left and I opened the door of the car for Delores, I said, "This could be the perfect house for us, Delores. Did you like it?"

"I loved it. You're right, this could be the answer to our prayers."

1000 Devonshire Road, Grosse Pointe Park, Michigan

"If we can swing the deal, we could be married in a month or two for the closing since we will have to be married in order to jointly sign the papers together as man and wife. Doesn't that sound nice? Man and wife."

"Just keep praying," Delores said. "Whatever will be, will be."

"We're sure are busy praying. I had never said a 54-day novena before. I didn't even know that they had these long novenas. I always thought they were only seven days. Well, when all else fails, keep praying, you and some saint said."

VIII

PLANNING

> *Not failure, but low aim, is a crime.*
>
> *J. R. Lowell 1819—1891.*

When I was a nine year old, my father died. Without a father, I remember I felt like a "second class citizen." Many times, I wished I had a father around like everyone else in my school, somebody to go home to and talk to every day. I surely missed my dad as I went through grade school and high school. I was in the third grade when my dad died. So, I knew that it's not easy for children to grow up with only one parent. My mother was a saint. I don't know how she managed to keep the family together. She sure knew how to stretch a dollar and make ends meet. But, I remember thinking that it would have been nice to know that I could take my problems to either one of two parents as most of my friends. It's nice if there are two parents to help children when they needed a helping hand as they grow up. One parent alone with the burden of raising children is a heavy responsibility of making all the decisions in planning, organizing, and control of children.

Later, after leaving the Army, when I was still young and before I was ever married, I use to think: To be average is a desirable goal. The average man does pretty well for himself in this great American land of plenty. He lives a pretty good life working eight hours a day and five days a week. He eats three meals a day and has his home and a car to drive around. He pays his taxes and takes a vacation every year. My dad died at age 42, the average man lives to about 65.

Yes, the average man lives a pretty good life, so if I can be average, that's better than my dad and I'll be satisfied with average." That was my thesis for the good live.

But, when Marge died, and I was left alone with seven children, all under twelve years old, and I was without their mother to help me raise them. Well, that's not average! Therefore, I thought to myself, if fate won't allow me to be average, then by God, I'm going to start being better than average … not less. That's why, when Marge died, I decided to go back to college and get my degrees. I decided that my new desire for more education would be based on a new axiom: *you can always do more than you think you can.*

I made many plans to change things and try to make something positive out of the disaster caused by her death. However, little did I realize that two years later there would be ten more children? Going back to college was also partially an escape mechanism to take my mind off of my torments. But, this continued education took on a greater significance when fate presented me with this new role as the father of seventeen children. I felt that it behooved me to continue the pursuit of that bachelor's degree as an example of the importance of education for my children. Now, even more than ever, I thought, I might also continue onto a master's degree. I set my aim to a higher goal. My aim was to be the best father these children would ever want.

Thus these plans for higher education and my endeavors to learn more would help me meet my obligation to be the best father possible. If my thesis on education was correct before, it was even more correct now. For example, even though I no longer needed the therapeutic value of study that I may have needed two years ago, I now felt that I should aspire to a better paying job just to support my large family with all the many additional bills.

Teamwork

The belief that God gives us talents and it's up to us to develop those talents and give them back to God a hundred fold is a biblical teaching. It's in the Bible someplace. I felt that to be the best father I would need all the help I could get from education and God. And, since my studies were in management and administration, I felt that these subjects would be very valuable to our success in this *joint venture* of marriage. We could put the things I learned to practical use right at home. But more importantly, I was lucky to have Delores, who was an able and wise homemaker and manager, willing and happy to manage the home with seventeen children while I would be attending classes two to three nights a week. This was just one more reason for me to endeavor even harder. Delores made all the difference in the world. Teamwork is the key. Success is easier with two working together in this crazy mixed up world. Another axiom: *behind every good man there's a better woman.*

It's a big job for two people and much more for one person alone. Many can't cope with it. They end up with nervous breakdowns or, worse, they take to drinking and become alcoholics. The children are the big losers. They not only suffer the loss of a parent but they are sometimes left to shift for themselves in this world that turns cold against them. Yes, the job of raising a family is much easier when there are two loving parents working together. So, getting married to a widow with ten children was an opportunity for me to pursue happiness for others. It was my privilege and honor, especially when it was *this* woman and *these* children.

IX

MARRIAGE: THE SECOND TIME AROUND

> *Were a man not to marry a second time,*
>
> *It might be concluded that his first wife*
>
> *Had given him a disgust for marriage; but*
>
> *By taking a second wife, he pays the highest*
>
> *Compliment to the first by showing that she*
>
> *Made him so happy as a married man that*
>
> *He wishes to be so a second time.*
>
> Samuel Johnson—1709-1784

I think marriage is God's way of forcing us to think of somebody else and taking our minds off ourselves. Children are God's way of further forcing us to continue to think of others and to further stop thinking of ourselves. I think that happiness is doing something for somebody else. The ego and the id are very poor companions in this journey through life that we find ourselves in this world. They can cause us a lot of unhappiness and stress. They even can destroy us if we let them. So, I think that the most important thing to do when you're sad is to *do something for somebody quick.* And that's what fate did for me after my devastation. It forced me to change my focus from myself to others. I think that "fate" and "god" are in close proximity.

X

THE WEDDING

I read the newspapers to see how God governs the world.

John Newton 1801-1890

My brother in-law, Patrick J. Foley, the brother of my first wife, Marge, was our attorney in the sale of our existing houses and the purchase of our pending new home. Pat called me a few days after we had signed the purchase agreement on the house at 1000 Devonshire.

"George," Pat said. "I just got word from the realtor that the owners have changed their mind and they are withdrawing the purchase agreement."

"They can't do that," I said. "What are they talking about?"

"They're talking about attempting to get out of the deal and not sell you the house."

"They can't do that," I repeated. They signed the purchase agreement."

"Yes, you're right. But, they're trying to break the contract if we let them."

"Well, we're not going to let them. This is the perfect house for the seventeen and I'm not going to spend another six months looking again."

"That's what I thought you'd say," Pat agreed. "But I wanted to hear it from you first."

"Why do they want to renege now, two weeks before the wedding?"

"I don't really know for sure. But, I have a suspicion that they received a better offer by someone else that would buy the house and the vacant lot next door. In short the answer is more money!"

"Well, it's too late. Tell them *no way!* They can sell the lot but not the house. The house is already sold to us."

"OK, I'll take care of it," Pat said as he hung up the phone.

The owner had been trying to sell the house and the lot together. We had offered to buy the house alone. The corner lot was priced at about forty percent of the cost of the house. We could only afford to buy the house as we had planned in our budget analysis. We didn't need the lot. We did need the house.

A few days later, Pat Foley called back and said, "Well, the deal is on again. The owners are going to go through with the purchase agreement and sell you the house to you as agreed."

"How did you manage to convince them?"

"Easy! I just told their lawyer that when we walk into court, I will have seventeen children following me into the courtroom."

"That was all you said?"

"Yes! That was all I said. It took all the fight out of him. He knew he had no chance."

"All right! Nice job, Pat. Keep up the good work."

Preparations

Preparation for our wedding included outfitting the two families in their Sunday best. That called for a "full dress *class A*" uniform inspection, referring back to my army days, and review by the commanding officers, Delores and me. After checking the seventeen for suits, blazers, shoes and dresses we began to issue the necessary attires. Delores volunteered to sew all the girls' new dresses.

These dresses were to be *hand-made* and not *homemade* by Delores. Hand-made implies the skill of a seamstress, whereas, homemade implies the product of an amateur. Luckily, Delores was a talented accomplished seamstress along with her other talents, so the new dresses were perfect.

One family with nineteen members led to what I call a multiple *progression* phenomenon. Everything from now on would have to be considered in multiples. We could not buy one child a present without buying all seventeen children a present. The budget cost of anything and everything would have to stand the test of *multiple progressions* in our budget. This phenomenon of multiplicity would reoccur over and over again in the months and years to come. But, one of the rewards was that our happiness as a family would also be multiplied. This was an advantage that the children would always cherish as time went by.

June 10, 1966

The date for the wedding was set for Friday morning, June 10, 1966. Father Sweeney, the pastor of St. Clare of Montefalco Church in Grosse Pointe Park, would say the mass. We chose Friday for the wedding so that we could have the weekend for the honeymoon trip and I would use the minimum amount of vacation time from work.

We also chose June 10 because we had the all-important closing date for the house six days later. This gave us five days for our planned honeymoon trip to Canada. We could not jointly get a mortgage for the new house until we were man and wife. Thus, the closing requirements for purchasing with the new bank mortgage had to be preceded by our wedding.

It was eight o'clock in the morning of our wedding day when I received a phone call at my house in Allen Park. It was a reporter from the Detroit News. Someone had called them and told them that Delores and I were getting married this morning. They wanted to verify the facts about the wedding and the circumstances. I later was told by Dick Wolff, a very good friend of Delores, that he had told his brother, Joe Wolff, a journalist at the Detroit News about the wedding. I guess that when a man and women take on seventeen young children, that's news.

The morning of our wedding was a beautiful, bright and sunny day. No wonder a lot of people has their weddings in June. The perfect month for our wedding … it was not too hot and not too cold, just right. If the start of our wedding day was any omen, we could expect a beautiful and happy future for our family. I even heard the birds singing and the flowers were never more beautiful … blossoms everywhere.

June rhymes with moon, spoon, and tune. June has the most sunny days and mild weather. It's so nice to have this beautiful weather after a long winter. And, like the song says … *just when your poor old heart can't go on, it seems; June brings a basket full of dreams*. And, that was what we had on our wedding day. We had a basket full of dreams.

St. Clare De Montefalco

As we had arranged, I drove my children to Delores' house on the morning of the wedding and after the final inspection, we would all get into our two station wagons and drive to St. Clare De Montefalco Church for the wedding. Delores and I had our hands full making sure that everyone was presented at their best for the mass. The children were all excited with anticipation. Participation in the wedding ceremony included all 19 of us as Delores had planned. When Delores' sister, Patricia, asked our two three-year olds, "Who's getting married this morning?" Little Mary Ann

McMillan and little Janet Arsenault both answered, "we are! All of us."

They were right. We were all getting married. One big happy wedding makes one big happy family. That was our prayer. This was a storybook wedding. This was a wedding where the bride and groom's children would all be in the wedding and they would all participate, each one marching down the aisle to the front of the church just as Delores had planned it. We wanted unity and togetherness and it would start right from the beginning. It would not be *your children and my children*. It would be *our children*. They would all be *our children* right from the beginning.

Delores' four older boys, Donald, Bob, Tim and Joe, seventeen, sixteen, fifteen and fourteen respectively, would be on the altar assisting Father Sweeney in the Mass ceremony while the two seven-year-old look alike, Susan McMillan and Aileen Arsenault, were the flower girls. All the rest preceded us down the center aisle. All the children were dressed up in their best. Many had new shoes and all had something new. It was quite a glamorous showing.

Notoriety

All morning long, at my house in Allen Park and at Delores' house in Grosse Pointe Park, the newspaper reporters kept calling and asking questions. "Is it true that you're getting married? Is it true that there are seventeen children between you? Is it true that you are joining two families to make a family of nineteen?" Now, in front of the church as we were going in for the ceremony, there they were, still asking questions but talking to our friends and relatives. They were talking to everyone it seemed. We had taken a low profile approach to the news media for the children's sake. But it seemed that everyone was interested in our *joint venture*.

The wedding ceremony went like clock work as Delores' careful planning paid off, one more indication of her talent as a great manager and organizer. As the last of the children were sent up the center aisle ahead of us, Delores said, with a twinkle in her eye, "I'm not going through with it. I've changed my mind."

"Delores," I said. "I hope you're kidding?"

"Yes, I'm kidding," as she took my arm and started us down the center aisle.

All went well without a hitch as we promised to *love one another until death does us part.* Everyone did his or her part in the wedding and we tied the knot firmly. After the ceremony, we all gathered on the steps in front of the church. The photographers were snapping our pictures before, during, and after the ceremony. My brother, Albert, and Delores' brother, Bob Shmina, were busy with their cameras taking pictures of the occasion. We had *stills* and *home movies* to remember the day. We also had the reporters and their photographers taking pictures as all nineteen members of this new Arsenault-McMillan family were exiting the church. Standing on the steps of the church together, the photographers were directing us to move over or stand here or there as they focused their cameras around us.

Little did we realize that the Detroit News and the Detroit Free Press would have our picture and story on their front pages the very next day, big as life?

St. Clare of Montefalco Church—June 10, 1966—
Wedding Day

Family in front of St. Clare Church

Front row girls: Ann McMillan, Margaret Arsenault, Janet Arsenault, Sue McMillan, Mary Ann McMillan, Aileen Arsenault. Second row boys: Joe McMillan, Patrick Arsenault, Martin McMillan, Steve McMillan, Mark Arsenault, Robert Arsenault. Third row: Donald McMillan, Mary Ann Arsenault, Patricia McMillan, Timothy McMillan (behind Patricia), Delores Arsenault (mother), H. George Arsenault (father), Robert (Jaimen) McMillan.

The Flower Girls

My brother, J. Albert Arsenault, was our Usher and Aileen and Susan were the flower girls.

Four church girls

Left to right: Ann Louise McMillan, Susan Jane McMillan, Margaret
Elizabeth Arsenault, Aileen Therese Arsenault

The Associated Press picked up the picture and the story and all the papers published the event. We later discovered that we made the newspapers from New York to Florida. We even received a clipping of our picture and story from a Texas newspaper. "All the world's a stage," I thought. When I was driving to Grosse Pointe, the car radio played songs like *People, Strangers in the Night* and *Follow Your Dream* from the popular movie *The Sound of Music.* I felt that this was omen and I thought that this *joint venture* is bound to work. Everything seems to point us in that direction. I felt that this was more of the writing on the wall. To add to the positive signs, while our family pictures was being taken on the front steps of the church, we were told that Delores' dad and mother were discussing with each other that with Delores' new additional seven children, they would now have thirty five grandchildren. It was nice to hear such positive remarks and acceptance by the grandparents.

The plan for our honeymoon was to stay overnight in downtown Detroit at the then new Pontchartrain Hotel. The next morning, we would drive to Toronto, Canada where we would stay overnight and then fly to Montreal leaving our car at the airport.

When we arrived in Montreal, my cousin, Gilberte Bujold, told us she saw our picture on their evening television news. Needless to say, we felt like celebrities as a result of all this publicity. In Montreal, we made a short visit to my two aunts who were nuns at the convent house of the teaching Sisters of the Holy Cross. Aunt Lydia and Aunt Estelle (sisters of my mother) were delighted. They assured us that the children and we were in their prayers. Then, after a day of visiting, we took a train out of Montreal to Toronto and pick up our car at the airport after staying overnight at the airport motel.

The following day, we drove to the boarder crossing over the bridge to Buffalo on the American side and on to Cleveland for another overnight stay in Cleveland. The following day was Wednesday when we would drive home in time for the closing.

We had to be home by Thursday to sign the papers as 'man and wife' for our new home. Actually, we were anxious to get home to the family. There were so many things for us to do, most of all the planning and preparing for the big move.

XI

IMPLEMENTATION

> *Where we cannot invent, we may at least improve.*
>
> Charles Colton 1780-1832

"Where would nineteen people sleep in one house?" That was the question of the day. We had designated the four main bedrooms in the front of the house as the girls' rooms, two in each bedroom. Delores and I would have the large master bedroom with our own bath. The oldest two girls would share the smaller master bedroom with its own bath and stall shower. Although the house had seven bedrooms and four full baths on the second floor, two of the bedrooms along the north wing section were originally servants' rooms or maids' quarters with a bath at the end of the hall, but the bedrooms were small and hardly enough room for nine boys. The servants' quarters had a door separating it from the rest of the house.

Luckily, the third floor was just as large as the second floor and also with high ceilings so we were able to build two large dormitory bedrooms for the nine boys. For the first month, they would bunk in the servants' quarters until we had finished putting up installation and paneling, complete with doors, hallway, and lighting on the third floor. The nine boys couldn't wait for it to be finish so that they would have more room. The five younger boys, Patrick

Arsenault, Marty McMillan, Mark Arsenault, Steve McMillan, and Robert Arsenault would share one of two large room (17' x 25') and the four oldest boys, Donald, Robert, Timothy, and Joe (all McMillans), would share the other large room. Each room had a built in desk with light for studying. The four older boys had a large closet and the five younger boys each had footlockers and an open clothes closet. That was our plan.

But, the city building inspector told me that he would not approve the construction plans for third floor occupancy until we put in a fire escape from the third floor. There were two windows on the third floor, one in each new room. At the furthest window from the stairway, we installed a thirty-foot chain escape ladder that was bolted to the windowsill and unfolded out to the ground. We made a 8mm home movie demonstrating the unfolding and use of this emergency exit. The two oldest boys, Donald, and Bob McMillan, were the stars of this movie and did the honors of demonstrating the ladder's use. Strict orders were given that this ladder would be used only in an emergency. Hopefully, it would never be used. Because of our limited budget, the family except for the electrical revisions and modernization of the kitchen did all the work. Delores', father A. Z. Shmina & Sons, donated the insulation of the third floor.

The kitchen renovation resulted after identification of the problems by asking such questions as: How does one feed nineteen people every day? Who does the planning and cooking? Who will do the cleanup after each meal? Do we have the right tools in the kitchen to do the job? Although the house was in very good condition, the house was forty years old and the kitchen somewhat antiquated. It had a very large industrial size gas stove made of iron. There was a very old canopy vent over the stove that dominated the kitchen. There was a sink in the main kitchen and a small sink in the butler's pantry, a room next to the kitchen. Each sink had a window over it. The butler's pantry had cabinets for dishes on both sides of the room. We felt that since the kitchen would be of prime importance every day and Delores' main work area, it should be modernized with all the latest conveniences. The old kitchen was not very functional for our purposes and therefore all approved the proposal for a new kitchen. A plan to refurbish and modernize the kitchen was solicited from a contractor. Mutschler Kitchens, of Grosse Pointe, was called on to do the job. It had a good reputation around Grosse Pointe of being the best and had been recommended to us. We would use the money we received for our wedding to start the job. The plan called for the replacement of the old refrigerator, stove, and sinks with new fixtures that would include a new refrigerator, double electric ovens, plus an electric range and a large microwave oven.

This new kitchen would have a built-in range with double self-cleaning ovens, built-in large capacity dishwasher, and refrigerator with a large freezer compartment. The basement would also have a refrigerator, a freezer cabinet, and a stove salvaged from our old homes. The butler's pantry would be refurbished with a partial wall removal to form an island for the stove and double oven and a bar with four stools that would serve four children. Next to the kitchen was the large breakfast room. This room would easily accommodate the remaining fifteen persons at its long breakfast table. The table had five chairs on one side and six chairs on the other side plus two chairs at each end of the table. Fifteen would sit at the main table for dinner and four would sit at the bar. The ones at the bar would be those that were late, volunteers or those that were designated for infractions of the rules and paying their penalty. Since two of our boys would be in the seminary, only two need be at the bar.

It was a hard and fast rule from the very beginning that all would assemble for the daily main meal and all would eat together. This main event at the end of each day would allow us all to share the day's experiences. It would facilitate the daily review of the pertinent plans and problems listed under old and new business. It was our method of communication at this informal family meeting. All were members of the *board* and were expected to attend. We had strict rules about all of the family being present and on time for the evening meal. Delores would plan preparations early in the day. Evening dinner was a symbol of family unity. Favorite dishes, some taking many hours to cook, were brought to the table steaming hot. Delores liked everything piping hot.

The evening dinner was more than just a good time to enjoy good food; it was an occasion to share the day's events and to talk about the things that mattered most to the family. This was the occasion and time that we would plan annual vacations or other outings. This was a time to laugh at someone's silly jokes and offer suggestions to solve someone's special problems. It was a time to be together in a very special way that would benefit all the family.

Delores was the chief cook and homemaker. On our income tax returns, she was designated under the caption *occupation* as a *homemaker. Not* a housewife, her job was a *homemaker.* This was very important. She made it her job to plan each day's meals and to prepare each day's dinner to be served promptly at 6 p.m. She delegated tasks to everyone in the family. The eight girls would share in the serving and cleanup after the meal. Delores' plan worked very well. The girls paired off and each pair would take turns at different tasks. The boys would be responsible for maintaining the grounds outside, both winter and summer. Sections of the outside were assigned to each from a partitioning map of the areas.

Most of the meals were baked, broiled, or boiled. There was very little frying. Meat loaves, meatballs, hamburger patties, spaghetti, chicken, our butcher's city-chicken, and his mock chicken were especially liked. Baked hams and roast beefs with mashed potatoes were among the favorites meals. The roast beef, mashed potatoes and gravy were always a big winner.

When we were planning our wedding, Fisher Body Fleetwood was modernizing its kitchen at the plant. When I found out that they were going to replace all the equipment and fixtures, I called the Salvage Department at General Motors and asked if I could buy the meat slicer. When they heard about the seventeen children, they saw to it that I got the slicer. It was this butcher's slicer that made it easy to serve nineteen people roast beef or ham. I could slice it as thin as I wanted and we were always able to make it go around. Another favorite was Delores' beef barley soup. She did wonders with six pounds of ground beef. Six pounds meant quarter-pounders for everyone and some left over for seconds.

Steaks

We rarely had steak for dinner ... not only because of the expense but also because of the difficulty in preparing nineteen steaks. However, once, my brother gave us a box of frozen steaks for a family treat. The children were all excited and let out the word in the local neighborhood that the Arsenault/McMillans were having steak for dinner tonight. Everyone, up and down the block, knew that George and Delores with their seventeen children would be having steak for dinner that night. As it turned out, the steaks were very tough. The children were busy trying to cut, chew, and swallow their steaks. They started to ask, "Is this steak?"

"Yes, this is steak. Do you like it?"

"No, I don't like it."

"Neither do I," one after the other said.

We had very few requests for steak after that experience. In fact, there are some of the children who today, many years later, still do not like steak. They would rather have hamburger then steak.

Saturdays and Sundays were days off for the chief cook and homemaker. So, it was *catch as catch can* for all. We always had cereal, milk, water, soups, sandwiches, and leftovers for everyone. The rule was: Eat when you're hungry but don't leave a mess.

We also tested the idea whether buying a half a cow for the freezer in the basement would be more economical. We discovered that cattle sold for freezers are usually a better grade and therefore, cost a little more than super market meat on sale. Also, there are many steaks and only a few roasts. We had the steaks ground into hamburger but that made our hamburger rather costly.

After our experience with one half a cow, we decided that it was more economical to buy our hamburger and roasts from the super market or a local butcher when they had sales. We found a butcher who knew about the seventeen children and he would tell us about his special sales. The lesson we learned from all this was that those who want top grade steaks and lots of convenience from shopping for meat could freeze a *half a cow* but it will cost them a little more and they will eat more meat. Our way was less expensive and less meat.

Bread

Another item on which we were able to save money but still have quality was bread. We estimated that we would use about five loaves a day. Bread came in twenty-sliced loaves and if we had seventeen sandwiches for the school lunches that would add up to 34 slices of bread. Many would take two sandwiches and we used up three loaves of bread for lunches. The daily ritual included the school milk money for fifteen plus, Delores would insist, each lunch must also include a piece of fruit and a cookie. Breakfast and dinner would also require bread and we used up another two loaves, if not more. Therefore, the *multiple progression phenomenons* were at work again. That also meant that we could use up to fifty loaves of bread every ten days.

I located a Silver Cup bakery on the east side of Detroit on Chene and Mack Avenue and they would sell *surplus bread* every day at a discount. I would pass Chene on East Jefferson every day on my way to and from work at the GM Fleetwood Plant. Many times, I was able to buy as much as seven loaves for a dollar. Normally, I would only get four loaves for a dollar. Our freezer in the basement would hold about fifty loaves of bread. So, I would buy fifty loaves every ten days. I believe the freezer bread was even fresher when thawed than bread not frozen.

When we were low on cereal, toasted *bread* would be the choice. Sometimes, Delores would make French toast and we would use up more bread. Delores had a counter in the kitchen that she had designated for the school lunches. Every evening, prior to a school day, Delores would place three rows of napkins, six columns across on this counter. The school milk money was placed on each napkin. An apple or a piece of fruit was added with a napkin and a paper bag. This was the routine that Delores prepared each night before school. In the morning, the older girls had the task of making the sandwiches. There would be special orders for bologna or peanut butter and jam, or some other lunchmeat. The sandwiches were made on a production-line method where one would put the bread down; another would deal out the lunchmeat, mustard, lettuce and etc. On some occasions, there would be complaints that they got the wrong lunchmeat or no lunchmeat at all. Those complaints were sent to the complaint department and the management took it up with the workers … encouraging them to improve their quality controls.

Milk

Milk was another important item. How much milk do we need? And, where do we buy the milk? This was before 'skim' and '2%' milk and the time when everyone was talking about too much fat in milk. Milk was necessary for morning cereal. Cereal was a good nutrient and vitamin supplier and it had a low per serving cost factor but it required milk. Delores discovered powdered milk. Borden's powdered milk was the big rage to cut down the fat in milk. However, nobody liked the taste of powdered milk. Delores solved this problem by using one gallon of whole milk and one gallon of powdered milk. Mixing it together and you had the lower fat content and the taste was great. So, we would buy two gallons of whole milk and mix them with two gallons of watered powdered milk. Thus we would have four gallons of 'low fat' milk. Also, Delores decided that at the main meal, water would be served and not milk. This helped everyone to drink more water based on the medical advice that the average person should drink ten glasses of water a day.

Many more questions in our search to identify problems needed asking, such as, "who does the washing?" and "who does the shopping?" or "how do you keep track of seventeen children?" We searched for answers but, since all the members of the family were eager to make a success of this venture and all were working to help in any way that they could, we were confident that these and other questions, would be satisfactorily answered and *domestic tranquility* and happiness would prevail in our new *blue heaven.*

XII

NUMBERS

> *The heavens themselves, the planets, and this centre,*
> *observe degree, priority, and place, course, proportion,*
> *season, form, office, and custom, in all line of order.*
> Shakespeare 1564-1616.

The rights and privileges of each family member are no small matters when they involve a family of seventeen children. After careful study and analysis, we decided that the ruling factor for rights and privileges would be seniority. Since the parents had the most seniority, they would be the managers. We would try to rule much like Socrates' *philosopher king* and thus wisdom and knowledge, derived from study and experience, would be given priority. Many questions such as: Who sits where at the table? Who sits next to the window in the car? Who drives the car?; Who is in charge when the parents are away?; would be answered by *seniority*. The unions at GM and other companies use seniority to solve all types of problems and we felt it would work for us. Seniority allowed us to be fair to all.

Donald McMillan was the oldest and he became number one in seniority among the children. Everyone could count off his or her number in rank by seniority. Little Mary Ann McMillan, our three year old, was number seventeen. The school lunches and clean laundry were sorted 1 to 17. Clean laundry would be folded and put into 17 piles on a large table near the two washing machines and dryers. Delores took our own washing up to our room. But the children were expected to pick up their "piles" and take them to their rooms, putting them away in their closets and drawers. For the school lunches, one kitchen counter was used for setting up the lunches the night before. Since Bob and Donald McMillan were away at school, five columns and three rows of napkins and milk money would start the lunches for the next day. Sandwiches were made in the morning by Delores' helpers and place at the appropriate place. It was an easy way to identify who ordered the peanut butter sandwich and who got the bologna sandwiches.

This numbering system facilitated all communications. The main telephone was a wall-phone in the kitchen. When calls came in for any of the boys who were usually on the third floor, we would have to send someone up to get them. The nine boys were usually on the third floor where they studied, read, slept, and calling up to the third floor every time someone got a call was a problem. It was difficult to tell someone on the third floor that they had a call on the first floor. Also, when supper was served, the message had to go to the third floor for all the boys. We decided that we would install a buzzer on the third floor, which was activated in the kitchen. The main laundry chute, about two feet square, came down from upstairs and a door in the kitchen opened to this laundry chute which was right next to the wall phone. We ran a wire up to the third floor inside this laundry chute. Whenever calls for the boys came in, all we had to do was open the laundry chute door and buzz them by number.

The buzzer facilitated our communications for the boys on the third floor. In fact, you could hear these buzzes all over the house including the basement because of the laundry chute. We used a 1 to 9 numbering system for the nine boys. The oldest of the boys was number one and the youngest, Steven, was number nine. Luckily, most of the phone calls were for the older boys and we only had to buzz once for Donald or twice for Bob. This method worked quite well. For supper, we would simply give a whole series of buzzes.

However, there were times when we called the ninth son, Steve, that meant nine buzzes and this confusion caused more than one to come downstairs, especially if it was near suppertime. When the supper call buzzes were heard, (nine plus) all the boys would come running down the back stairway. No one wanted to miss supper.

We also used the use a numbering system in the laundry room. Delores would average eight loads of laundry each day. She would put two loads in the two washers every morning before breakfast and when the washer buzzed at the finish, she would put these two loads in the two dryers and start two new loads in the washers. This would continue through out the day. As the washing came out of the dryer, it was folded and put on a large table according to the numbers. The children were responsible for picking up their laundry and putting it in dresser drawers and hangers. They were also responsible for the cleanliness of their rooms and sending soiled clothing down the center hall chute on the second floor to the basement. This was a very large chute with a large three feet square box in the basement laundry room to catch the clothes.

Someone once said, "you cannot teach a child to take care of himself unless you let him try to take care of himself." This we did. The children were required to pick up their laundry at the large table in the basement laundry room. Socks and clothes were initialed with white thread by Delores to identify the owners.

Sometimes, some piles of clean clothes would get bigger and bigger which meant the owner was not picking up their laundry. We would wonder what that person was wearing. We did not notice anyone wearing dirty clothes. It became obvious that some were using the laundry room table for storage instead of transferring the clean clothes to their dressers. They preferred to go to the basement and take what they needed to wear at any given time. This situation led to an announcement on the family large bulletin board that read *Pick up your laundry now number 7 and number 4 or else.*

Delores never told me what the *or else* was, but I'm sure everyone else knew or at least they did not want to find out.

The ability to communicate an infraction of rules by number had the gracefulness to get the message across without being personal or demeaning. However, if this notice did not result in remedial action, the next step was to mention names after which there would be a one-on-one confrontation.

Friends would ask if there was any confusion with the numbers and there was some. Our children were not just numbers. But somehow this sequential system worked to solve many problems. With a little thought, they could identify anyone's number. Even Delores and I had to refer to our list occasionally to get the right number. The first number and the last number were easy but sometimes the others took a little effort. Did all the children feel comfortable knowing that they had a number? Yes, I believe so. They knew the number represented their position in the seniority sequence. They all knew that they were more than just a number. I think that they also appreciated the convenience the numbers gave them in solving some of our problems.

All the children even applied the numbers in a matter-of-fact manner both at home and in school. We were told by one of the children's teachers at school, during the parents—teacher's conferences, about an incident that happened shortly after little Mary Ann, one of our five-year-olds, started school. It seems that when Mary Ann started the first grade at St. Clare grade school, which was the same school that eight of her brothers and sisters were attending, her teacher, who was familiar with our family merger, asked her, "Well, so you're one of the Arsenault—McMillan family. And which one are you?"

"I'm number seventeen!" little Mary Ann McMillan happily replied.

Superstition

That single number 'seventeen' kept re-occurring everywhere we turned. We are not superstitious but it was interesting to note how that certain numbers kept popping up over and over and sometimes in the most unusual places. I agree with the French philosopher and writer Jean Rousseau (1712-1778) who said, "I think we cannot too strongly attack superstition." But, I also agree with the English philosopher Francis Bacon (1561-1626) who said 150 years before Rousseau, "There is a superstition in avoiding superstition." So, it seems to me that taken in the light of these two great thinkers, that as long as superstition does not dominate decisions and life then these coincidences of events can be acceptable for what they are, an interesting and amusing comparisons of coincidental events.

It was in this light that we took note of the number seventeen and its frequency and repetitiveness of its appearance. I half-jokingly called this curiosity and coincidence to Delores' attention as the *writing on the wall*. I suggested that it was God's approval of our joint venture in marriage to raise these beautiful seventeen children. Be that what it may, we were always amazed to find another repetition of the number seventeen as we went about the business of raising this family.

It is interesting to note that the Bible has a whole book called *Numbers*. The Bible also speaks of the *seven days to build the world* if you count the *day of rest*. There were the *twelve* tribes of Israel and the *ten* lost tribes. The New Testament talks about the *twelve* apostles; the *three* persons in *one* God; Christ's *forty* days in the desert and the resurrection of Christ in *three* days. It goes on and on, and numbers with God seem to go together. We all would like God to give us a sign for direction. The Jews asked Moses for a sign from God when they doubted him. The *Ten Commandments* were written in stone by the *finger of God*. So, when the number seventeen kept appearing, it was easy for us to make some sort of evaluation and interpret this to be a sign from God that we were on the right track.

The seventeen miles of expressway from Allen Park to Grosse Pointe Park was the first occurrence. With some thought, I discovered that my phone number, 331-2710, added up to 17. Also, our car license numbers, BWK737 and LSX539, both added up to 17. The first apartment that I rented when I married Marge was 1707 Livernois in Detroit. My father's barbershop address was 717 Junction Avenue in Detroit. I'm not superstitious, but, as I often repeated to Delores, those number coincidences were so prevalent and frequent that I thought that if we had not gotten married and made a go of this merger, a bolt of lightning might have come down from heaven and struck both of us. It seemed to be our destiny.

On our first night after being married, the room at the Pontchartrain Hotel was 1017. It's nice to have everything working for you and it's nice to feel that God is on your side and helping you. *Nothing succeeds like success* when all your plans work out. I've discovered that it's not *Murphy's Law* that holds *if something can go wrong, it will and at the worse possible time.* No it's not Murphy's Law, it's the *devils.* That sneaky devil is always trying to make life miserable for all and blaming it on somebody else. Even during World War II, the *gremlin* was another name for the devil and I remember the situation always was summed up as *snafu* (situation normal, all fouled up.) But, I think it was the devil that *fouled up* all the time. It's nice to think that God's on your side once in a while and he puts a stop to the sly diabolical antics of the devil.

XIII

UNITY

Men's hearts ought not to be set against one another,

But set with one another, and all against evil only.

Thomas Carlyle 1795-1881

As I have stressed, family unity was one of our primary goals. So we were not only seeking *unity* for the strength derived from it, but unity in the love and understanding with compassion for one another as a family of brothers, sisters, and parents. We agreed that we needed *unity of command* as parents so that the children could not pit the father against the mother or vice versa. We did away with *ask your mother* or *ask your father* and *wait till I tell your father* or *wait till I tell your mother*. We agreed to make decisions together. As Abraham Lincoln stated in his speech at the Republican State Convention in Springfield, Illinois on July 17, 1858 (note the month and day is 717) "A house divided against it cannot stand." He was quoting Christ from the Bible (Mark 3:25.) "… And if a house be divided against itself, that house cannot stand." So, we felt that one of our tasks would be to create an atmosphere of one united family

The family is an entity like a corporation that can succeed or lose together. For example, if the father gets a raise or promotion, then the family got a raise or promotion. It's not just one person. Also, if you want to be nice to me then be nice to my family. It works both ways. When you give something to a man who has a family, you're really giving something to the man *and* his family. This thesis also applies to the whole family. Be nice to each other and you're being nice to the parents. It's like Christ saying, "inasmuch as you did it for the least of my brethren, you did it for me." And so it goes. Luckily, our children always had a high regard for each other and many times they would come to the defense of each other. If I were to ask, "who broke the glass?" All were silent. No one snitched on the other. The children seemed to always be glad to help one another. I believe that they knew the value of unity and family. There is great comfort in knowing that you can always count on your brothers or sisters for help even if it's three o'clock in the morning and you're stuck somewhere on a lonely road. After all, if you can't depend on your own family, whom can you depend on?

We were always trying to teach our children right from wrong. Many lessons of value were found on our large bulletin board from time to time. The following two verses, *If You'd Like To Have* and *The Men in the Ranks* were favorites that many of the children learned by heart and can repeat to this day. In the first verse, <u>home</u> can be changed to <u>church</u>, <u>family</u>, <u>teacher</u> or <u>anything</u>:

IF YOU'D LIKE TO HAVE
If you'd like to have the kind of a <u>home;</u>
Like the kind of a <u>home</u> you'd like.
You needn't pack your cloths in a bag,
And start on a long-long hike.
For you'll only find what you left behind,
For there's really nothing new;
It's a knock at yourself when you knock your home.
It isn't your <u>home</u> … it's you!

THE MEN IN THE RANKS

There are men in the ranks,
That will stay in the ranks.
Do you know why?
I'll tell you why.
Simply because they haven't
The ability to get things done.

Here are samples of a few more of our bulletin board announcements and notices:

BE NICE
It's nice to be important,
But it's more important to be nice.

GET IT DONE
If you want something done,
Give it to a busy person.

And it will be done.

GET LUCKY
It's funny, but the harder you work;
The luckier you get.

GET TOUGH
When the going gets tough,
The tough get going.

Don't drink and drive.
Don't ride *with anyone who drinks and drives.*
Don't be a fool … Stay in school.
Birds of a feather flock together; so pick your own friends
Don't let them pick you.
If you want to know what kind of a person someone is,
Check out his friends.
Be careful whom you chose for a friend.

In our capacity as parents we took the role of personnel managers. We did a lot of clipping from magazines and newspapers for the family bulletin board. When we saw something that we thought would be especially timely and pertinent to our family, up it went on the bulletin board. Some items were on the bulletin board only a few days. Others stayed up longer. For example, there was a plaque that stated:

A day is wasted without laughter.

Other Plaques

The best thing I ever have in my kitchen
Is a friend that can cook. HELP WANTED.

Recipe for a happy kitchen;
A measure of good will,
A full cup of understanding;
Mix with joy,
And add plenty of love.

Bless this home and all who are in it.

True love is life's greatest treasure,
And it is a decision.

We also had some humorous signs that would occasionally find their way up on the family bulletin board.
Uncle Sam wants you!
Join the Navy and see the world.
Join the Peace Corps.
Become a priest.
Join a Nunnery.
Elope!
It's fun to run away.
Write if you find work.

I think that everyone of us has sometimes contemplated running away. We never really had any run-a-ways in our family except one. We would have been very hurt if anyone had really run away before the age of majority (whatever majority means.) Our children were just average among others but to us, as most parents, they were special. But, there was one incident when someone decided to run away. The story, as told by Delores, involves Marty when he was about seven years old. Years before our marriage, Marty had decided that he had had enough.

"I'm going to run away," Marty emphatically told his mother.

"Oh, is that right? Do you want me to help you pack?"

"No!"

"Well, let me know when you're leaving."

"Okay."

So, Marty went to his room and returned with a little suitcase, stating,

"I'm leaving now."

"Well, good-bye and write if you find work," his mother said.

Out the door went Marty. Unknown to Marty, one of the older brothers had been instructed by his mother to follow him and make sure that he didn't get lost or in trouble and that he didn't go too far. About ten minutes later, the front door bell rang. There was Marty with his suitcase.

"I want a ride," he demanded, "because I'm not allowed to cross the street."

"You get in here Marty!" his mother said. "It's almost supper time and I don't have the time to drive you. You'll just have to run away some other time."

Drugs & Alcohol

How did we deal with drugs and alcohol? That was a subject that we discussed frequently as a family. I would tell them "Don't be the one who gets drunk and have everybody laugh at you. When someone says to you 'man, I'm going to get drunk tonight,' he's really being ignorant. What he is really saying is 'I will dull my brain tonight, thus impairing my ability to see, hear, talk, walk, and think.' This is pretty dumb. He may as well say that he wants a brain tumor because the symptoms are the same. Once drunk, a person is vulnerable to attack and destruction by anyone sober since the ability to protect oneself is very noticeably impaired. A drunk becomes fair game for anyone who wants to take advantage of him. And, continued abuse of alcohol or drugs will deteriorate the body until finally your health degenerates into self destruction."

Drugs are just another form of self-abuse, except drugs are even more dangerous. These were some of the arguments that we used to warn our children about the use of drugs and alcohol. We tried to teach our children that they should avoid drugs like poison. Only at the prescribed direction of a doctor for the cure of illnesses should drugs be taken. It is ignorant to gamble on drugs for pleasure.

We also tried to teach moderation in all things. Excesses in anything and nature usually makes you pay a price. Even in over-eating, there's obesity that can lead to many illnesses and disabling diseases with an early death. Moderation is the key word for a healthy and, hopefully, a long life

Questions

When hearing that we had a large family, many friends would ask us, "How do you keep track of them?" Well, it wasn't easy. But, Delores developed a sixth sense about it. She could almost feel when someone was missing or not where he or she was supposed to be. Delores became very acute to sensing who was not in at night. She said that she never was able to sleep until everyone was in the house. Mothers are endowed with a special instinct to watch over their children. And the mother of seventeen had developed this instinct to a high degree of awareness and perception for the welfare of her children. This was all part of our good management and control.

We had a rule. Whenever anyone was out in the evenings, with permission of course, they were required to knock on our bedroom door when they got in if it was after we had gone to bed. It's not that we wanted to be awakened. It's just that we cared about them. If we did not care, we would never ask any questions and there would not be any rules. They could run wild. But, we did care and we do care ... very much so. That's why we had an *in and out* sheet on the family bulletin board. They were expected to sign *in and out* whenever they went somewhere other than school. There was a column for when they were expected back and where they went. This worked pretty well. The children were good about leaving this information. It also helped to be able to tell their friends when they would be home for callbacks.

Our teenagers were concerned with communicating and going out with their friends. However, sometimes they would have to answer certain questions about their comings and goings. When the teenagers who had driver's licenses would ask to borrow the car, they would have to answer some pertinent questions for this privilege of borrowing the car. The questions were as follows:

Where are you going?
With whom are you going?
How long will you be gone?
When will you return?
Is your homework done?
Is your room clean?

If they were able to satisfactorily answer these questions, permission and the car keys would be granted, but they were still required to sign out.

At times I felt that a rule of knocking on our bedroom door was carried a bit too far. In the middle of the night there would be a knock on our bedroom door waking me up. Delores would be awake waiting for that knock. One night I was awakened from my sleep by a knock on our bedroom door.

"Who's there?" Delores asked in a whisper.

"It's me. I'm home! Did I get any phone calls?" Someone whispered back.

"No. Good night and go to bed." Delores would answer in a tired manner looking at the clock to check the time.

"OK. Good night."

Then I would turn over and think to myself, "who was that? I bet it was Tim. I think he was the only one that was still out and would want to chitchat at this ungodly hour.

The next morning, I would interrogate Delores.

"Was it Tim that knocked on our door when he came in last night."

"Yes. We talked for quite a while."

"What time was it?"

"It was late."

A little later, Tim came down and sat at the breakfast table.

"What time did you knock on our door last night?" his mother would ask.

"I don't know," Tim answered, "but it was early."

"Early in the morning?"

"No, it wasn't. I remember that it was just around eleven thirty. And, by the way, can't I have my own house key?"

"No! We've got enough keys around here. Just remember to put it back on the key rack for someone else."

Notice the strategy and tactic used by Tim. When after collecting data, it was determined that no one knew for certain what time he came in, then, it was as always *around eleven o'clock*, the curfew hour for sixteen year olds. *Around* was a matter of interpretation. The next step was to quickly change the subject. "Why can't I have my own house key?" was a diversion tactic. There's no doubt. We had a lot of smart children.

Who gets their own key to the house? Everyone wants his or her own key. But, we decided that they would get their own key at the age of seventeen. Otherwise, they would have to use the spare key on the key rack. The *key* was a clear indication of our trust in their maturity and when given to someone, it meant that we were confident of their good sense of responsibility and trust. This thinking goes with the adage: *Give someone a good reputation and there's a good chance they will live up to it and not let you down.* It was just another lesson to learn when growing up in a large family.

Training

There are many lessons to be learned while growing up as a member of a large family and the opportunity for family unity and concern were not the only lessons. A large family gives everyone the chance to learn the art of getting along with others. How to win friends and get along with people can easily be learned from the in and out of daily living. Everyone was a different unique person with his or her own personalities. The task of everyone striving to understand and appreciate each other with each one's special talents was an everyday encounter. It was a matter of learning to give and take in appreciation and understanding that was learned by osmosis.

Delores often said, "A large family at home is the perfect training ground for human relations and personnel management. If a person can learn the lessons of living in a large family, then living with the outside world becomes a piece of cake." It was our premise that happiness is not measured by *how much you can do for yourself*, but by *how much you can do for others.* The training and opportunity for *doing something for somebody else* starts right in the home from the crib on up. Delores, who earned a bachelor's degree from Marygrove University, with a major in Early Education, knew that the training and love starts at birth and the first few years of a child are the most important for any child.

Delores had always wanted a large family and she felt that she could do a good job. She felt a large family was a great gift to give to her children as long as one could afford them. The advantage of many brothers and sisters added strength to each one. One can always turn to your brother or sister for help when needed. Growing up with a large family is not only a learning process for the children but also for the parents. It is interesting to observe that when parents finally get good at their job as parents and the children get good at their jobs as children it's all over and the time comes for the children in the family to leave and make their own way in this life. Thus, the cycle goes on as God has decreed, *a time for everything*. It is hoped that when the children leave, they will be better parents than we because they had the advantage of growing up in a large family. Many do not have that unique advantage when they were young.

XIV

MONEY

> *The use of money is all the advantage there is in having it.*
>
> Ben Franklin 1706-1790

Money and budget management are a very important part of our family planning and we included money management in our family teaching endeavor to our children. We wanted to initiate the children in what we thought was the correct and pragmatic approach to money. There are many axioms about money, all good and important to remember. For starters, Benjamin Franklin, (who became one of the most successful and wealthiest men in America) owned 18 paper mills, invented daylight saving time, discovered the Gulf Stream, invented the stove named after himself, bifocals, electric explosives, and the public libraries. He left us with a wealth of axioms about money, e.g.: *A penny saved is a penny earned; It's hard for an empty bag to stand upright. Most problems are money problems.*

My own mother, who called herself *just a farm girl* said, "it's not how much money you earn that makes the difference, it's how much money you save." She opened bank accounts for my brother and sister in our names when we were still young children.

Time is money it has been said. We spend 35 to 40 years of eight-hour days working for money. But, there are some things more important than money. Take *health* for example. Money without health is worthless. If our health fails, we would gladly spend our money to regain our health if we could. That's why we should plan for those golden retirement years when we will no longer have to trade our time to work for money. Careful money management and healthy habits in youth will allow us to have the time for our money later on. Benjamin Franklin said that during our working years, *most problems are money problems*, but, Ben Franklin had enough money to retire at the age of 42 and that's when he stopped working for money. He turned over all his business to his partner, David Hall, and for the next 42 years, he had the time and money to pursue all of his many interests in astronomy, politics, and inventions without worrying about money. He died at the age of 84, still a rich man. These were some of the thoughts and axioms that we tried to instill in our children.

Years ago, during the Great Depression of the late twenties and early thirties, everyone seemed to be out of work and looking for a job. The expression *write if you find work* became an expression used for people leaving their home looking for work. The search went to other cities and other states. People would go wherever there was work. Some even went to Alaska looking for gold. An older friend of mine went to Alaska looking for gold in 1933. He didn't find gold, but he did find work ... fishing. He said he found *the gold in salmon fish*ing.

These values and truism we tried to pass on to our seventeen children. As children, we go to school to learn the things that will help us find work. The better and more we learn, the better job we can get and the more money we will be able to make. That's part of life in the big city. We work to take care of our families and ourselves.

I have always felt that the value of a person was in the ability to work. It was not how much money he has, but it was in what a person was capable of doing. What value is money or good looks if you're lost on a desert island? The ability to do things and get things done increases the value of a person. A person is only worth what he can do for himself and for his friends. I believe that the ability to get constructive things done and to make a contribution to society is their own ultimate reward for hard work. I believe that we need to work just for our own mental health. Benjamin Franklin said, "An idle mind is the devil's workshop."

These were some of the thoughts and the philosophy that became part of our family philosophy. Old Ben Franklin once wrote, "*If you know how to spend less than you make, you have the philosopher's stone.*" We wanted to teach our children the habit of saving. And it is a habit. I would tell them to *always save ten percent of what you make. Pay yourself first.* Their grandfather, A. Z. Shmina, would give the children a five-dollar bill and tell them not to spend it. "Keep it for an emergency," he would say. He knew the value of money. He came to this country at the age of fifteen from Romania, which was part of the Ottoman Empire, with only five gold pieces that his father gave him. He worked in a restaurant washing dishes at night to get his degree as an engineer. He retired as chairman of the board of A. Z. Shmina & Sons Construction Company ... competing with Darin & Armstrong, Barton Mallow and other large construction companies.

So, from the very beginning, when the children would receive money for their birthdays or other reasons, Delores and I would tell them, "put it in the bank." From the very start of our *joint venture,* one of the first things that we did was to open bank accounts at the NBD Bank for each of the seventeen children. The older boys had paper routes and the older girls did baby sitting. The habit of saving was started at a very early age. Many of the children ended up with sizable amounts of money in their accounts, which helped them later during their college years. For example, Donald McMillan, our oldest, having won a scholastic scholarship to the University of Detroit, used his bank savings to buy his first used car, a Ford T Bird, and to pay for one summer of studies at Oxford University in England.

Delores would do all the banking and weekly she would take the seventeen bankbooks to deposit a dollar here and two dollars there into the individual accounts. The tellers at the bank would always ask the usual questions when they saw all the bankbooks:

"How do you manage such a large family?"
"Who does all the cooking?"
"Who does all the washing?"
"Who does all the cleaning?"
"How do you keep track of seventeen children?"
"I'll bet you could write a book."

Budgeting

All needs regarding expenditures for the household were always a joint decision. All major expenditures were carefully analyzed and studied. "Get three bids," I would always say. That was one basic requirement at GM for all project expenditures. I worked in property records and was knowledgeable of capital expenditures. In our joint-decision making, we took the same approach. We had the added advantage of our own expertise to contribute to the decisions. Delores was an expert homemaker and manager. I would do the bookkeeping and analysis. Incidentally, in the event of a bad decision, we would share the blame. No one person was at fault.

The study of budgeting, as I have said, played a very important role in our final decision to attempt this marriage. Uniting two large families as we did could never have succeeded without careful planning and management. We knew that. I had made several budget plans for our anticipated expenditures months before we were married just to convince ourselves that we could do it.

Our budgeting was based on the following thesis: It is important to think of a budget as a changing and dynamic planning document. It should always remain flexible and the ability to adjust budgets to current needs and events is very important. Budgeting can be viewed as a road map used to achieve planned objectives or goals. First, we set goals and objectives, and then decisions are made as to what priorities are used to get to goal. Sometimes there were many roads that could be taken. Style of living, income, fixed costs and variable costs would dictate the necessary decisions that must be made to attain budget goal objectives.

Budgeting is similar to the navigational art of *dead reckoning* that a sailor uses to set course and direction. It is based on all known factors that would affect the course and direction, such as wind direction, current speed, water depth, and compass readings. The *dead reckoning* course is adjusted and re-plotted from time to time as new data and information are collected. So is the planned budget. The budget was always adjusted as we made new decisions regarding priorities and needs.

Here are a few **axioms** that helped us make decisions as to our needs and necessities on our budget:

Whatever you can't afford is expensive at any price.
Save ten percent for yourself even if you have to borrow money.
A bad or incomplete budget plan is better than no plan at all.
Budgets are dynamic and change is inevitable.

Money Managers

People would sometimes ask, "How can you afford to send all your seventeen children to college?" The answer was, "We can't totally." But, in our family, anyone who wanted to go to college went to college. However, if we were to pay for the college education of seventeen children, we had to consider the high cost when the *multiple progression phenomenons* take effect. For example, if college tuition were two thousand dollars a month, we'd have to spend $34,000 for one year's college education. "Who gets what and how much," was a money management decision that we had to contend with every day. We have been guided by the thesis that *God helps those who help themselves.* We decided we would pay the initial costs for the first semester for anyone. If they chose a college near home, that would help reduce college expenses. They would get whatever Social Security allotted for them while they stayed in college. The McMillans also were eligible for a small amount that the Veterans Administration would pay if the children stayed in college up to the age of 21. They could get part time jobs and, when needed, we would give them some money to stay in college.

The children's grandfather, A. Z. Shmina, also gave them some money to help pay college expenses. The children were ambitious and worked not only part time jobs, but summer jobs. I was able to get some of them summer jobs at the Fisher Body Fleetwood Plant where I worked. These would be temporary jobs during the summer model-change-over but they would pay the wages that General Motors paid all production workers. All in all, somehow the children all learned to manage their money and were able to stay in college and work their way through. Also, our children discovered there are government loans, grants, and other financial aids available. So, *Budgeting* and *Money Management* were two of the all important lessons that we tried to teach our children while growing up in the *big house* with the *big family* in the *big city.*

XV

AUTOMOBILES

The sum of the whole is this: Walk and be happy. Walk and be healthy.

The best way to lengthen out our days is to walk steadily and with a purpose.

Charles Dickens 1812-1870

"The board meeting will come to order!" I said as we sat around the dinner table.

"Now, what is this problem about cars?"

"Well, I need the car to go to the football game," sixteen-year-old Tim, said.

"But I need it to go to the library," big Mary Ann said.

"What about me?" sixteen-year-old Patrick asked. "I need the car too."

"We can't afford cars for every driver," Delores said. "With the high school five miles away that's why we have a car pool. We have to share my car since Dad needs his car to go to work so that's not available."

"What we need is a special car for the children," I suggested. "Maybe this family needs three cars instead of two ... one for me to go to work, one for mother to do the shopping and run errands, and one for the children to share for a school car pool, the library, shopping, part time work, dates, and all the other reasons they have for borrowing their parents cars."

"Yea, that's what we need. Our own car," everyone chorused.

"It would be cheaper to insure a third small car for the children's exclusive use than to have them all listed and insured on our bigger cars," I said. "That way we could insure the large cars exclusively for the parents … one for work and one for pleasure."

Cars were a problem, as well as they were costly and they can be dangerous. When we first were married, we had four teenage drivers and two family cars. After a few minor accidents, some speeding tickets, and the demand to borrow our cars, we knew we had a car problem. What would we do when we knew we had thirteen more teenage drivers? What was the best way to solve the dilemma? The transportation needed serious and careful analysis to resolve it satisfactorily. Rule one of scientific decision making was to identify the problem. We had too many teenage drivers for only two cars. That was the problem. What's more, new drivers seemed to have frequent fender benders, speeding tickets and other infractions of the traffic laws. All these problems were brought to the dinner board meeting.

The questions I asked were always the same:

"Why did you get a speeding ticket and how can this be avoided?"

"What can we do to protect ourselves against these problems?"

The discussions helped everyone understand the problems that new drivers face. All learned a lot. Even those who were not yet drivers learned from these deliberations and discussions.

We had two large station wagons that the teenage drivers had to borrowed when they needed a car. Both were relatively new. Both had high-powered V8 engines. One of our drivers with four of his friends in the car got a ticket speeding eighty five miles an hour on a sixty-five-mile-an-hour expressway. How do we prevent this from happening again? That was the problem that led to a children's car.

The Opel

Delores and I decided that a smaller car was needed for the young drivers ... a car with less horsepower, a car that would not be allowed on the expressway by our orders, a car that would not be used for *joy riding, a* car that would be used only for trips to the library, school and for work. We found a good used four-cylinder four-door Opel station wagon. Our insurance costs went down when we took the teenage drivers off the big car and insured them only on the Opel, with no collision. The Opel had only liability insurance.

The tickets and fender benders stopped even as four more teenage drivers joined the teenage family drivers. It was a stick shift; so all had to learn to drive a stick shift. All went well until a car ran a stop street and drove into the side of our Opel, broad siding the wagon just hard enough to turn it over on its side. Luckily, the four girls in the car escaped injury because they were wearing their seat belts and neither car was going fast. Our teenage daughter, Ann Louise, the driver, and her three friends were on their way to the library when the accident occurred. The other driver's insurance company totaled the Opel and they paid us the salvage value of seven hundred dollars.

We kept the money as well as the car. We fixed the broken side windows with Plexiglas and bumped out the fenders. We hand painted the dents. So what are a few dents? With only these repairs, it was still good, cheap and dependable transportation. We were getting close to thirty miles to the gallon.

There were rules for use of this car, which included approval from the parents at all times. Sightseeing drives and touring were not allowed and drives on the expressways were definitely out. No one wanted to drive it faster then the thirty-five-mile-per-hour speed limit anyway because of the rattles in the car. Actually these rules were easy to follow because the way the car looked, rattled and shook, it was no pleasure when it went faster than twenty-five miles per hour. A new rule went up on the family bulletin board after the accident; *Wear your seat belts to remind you to drive safely.*

The whole episode turned out to be beneficial. The Opel looked like a wreck. But it solved our problems of teenage drivers and slowed them down. One look at the Opel and everyone was reminded to wear seat belts and drive safely. It was a stick shift and everyone had to learn to shift gears. The green Opel became a legend in its own time. It was seen all around the Grosse Pointes. It was seen at many high school homecoming parades with all kinds of water paints decorating the many dents. One of our daughters, Margaret Elizabeth, wrote an endearing poem about the Opel.

Opel Station Wagon

OUR DEAR OPEL CAR

Oh Opel car, how sad you look.
One side of you is all smashed.
Your passenger door doesn't open any more,
And you haven't been the same
Since you crashed.

You're only three,
To the world, you look ten.
To me, you look even older.
But, Opel dear, at heart you're young
Though physically,
You just get moldier.
In the winter I freeze,
In the summer I bake.
Though these hardships,
I hardly consider.
It's my friends who gripe.
Make unkind jokes and laugh,
When you cough and sputter.

So, Opel dear, take heart … don't fret;
You know we'll never desert you.
So long as your engine
Continues to gurgle,
Your brakes never fail,
When we need you.

XVI

DIVERSIONS

*The mind ought sometime to be diverted, that it may
return the better to thinking.*

Phaedrus 14-54 AD

Summer vacations were another consideration in our family
planning sessions. Everyone wanted the family to take a vacation
together. With nineteen persons in a family, where can they all go
together and still keep the costs reasonable? Cruises and flying
would be too expensive. How far can we go? A day's drive would be
the best we could expect. That meant someplace within four or five
hundred miles. Since my work only allowed two weeks vacation,
that would be the duration of our trip. Will everybody be going?
Everybody up to the oldest wanted to go.

These were some of the questions that were posed at the dinner table board meetings. After all, if other families went on vacation, why can't and shouldn't we? Being a big family was not a
good reason to be different from any other family when it comes
to vacations. A discussion was held at the dinner table with many
suggestions:

"All those who want to go on a vacation somewhere this summer
say aye," I said.

"Aye!" everyone answered.

"The *ayes* have it."

"Question: where do we want to go? The ocean, mountains, seashore, the Great Lakes or Alaska?"

"Alaska!" they all shouted.

"Just kidding. You'll have to go to Alaska on your own. I think we should stick to the Great Lakes. Michigan is a beautiful place for summer vacations."

"Let's just go somewhere," Delores said.

"I think a trip up north would be the most practical. What we need is a cottage that will sleep nineteen people."

"Where will we ever find such a cottage?" Joe asked.

"We'll have to start looking in the papers for cottages for rent and make some inquiries."

"I'll check the Grosse Pointe News for listings," Tish volunteered.

"Let's try to go to Burt Lake or somewhere on Lake Huron," I suggested.

"When we get some phone numbers, we can call the people and find out how many their cottages will accommodate. Maybe they can give us some suggestions," 'Big' Mary Ann said.

"Many times, cottages have a screened in porch with a few cots to accommodate more people," Mark added.

"And maybe we'll need two cottages," Delores said.

"They would need to be close to each other to be of any fun."

"I bet we could borrow a large tent from the Boy Scouts and we could go camping," Steve remarked.

"Sorry. Tents are not for me," Delores said. "I want hot and cold running water and a chrome-plated bathroom."

"This is our first vacation as a family of nineteen, and I don't think that a tent is the right answer," I said. We're going to be roughing it up enough as it is. Nice suggestion anyway, Steve."

"I think that a week up North at a Michigan Lake with two cottages next to each other would be great," Doc suggested.

It was agreed that we would search the papers for a couple of cottages up North and we would plan for a week on one of Michigan's lakes. Everyone was enthusiastic about the vacation and all wanted to go. Everyone started watching the papers for rental cottages. A day's drive would get us as far as the Mackinac Bridge. Our target would be somewhere near Topinabee at Burt Lake or Alpena on Lake Huron somewhere in Michigan.

We found a cottage at Burt Lake that had six bedrooms. It was really two cottages that had been connected together making one large family room and kitchen. There was a fireplace and plenty of wood in the woodpile. The rent was only two hundred dollars for a week. The owner said that he normally did not rent it except for a few weeks in the summer to help pay for upkeep. We decided to rent it for one week with the intention of adding a second week if all went well and we liked it.

"Where on Burt Lake?" Patrick asked when the news was announced at the dinner table.

"I looked it up," Doc said. "It's near Indian River where there's a shrine with the world's biggest crucifix. The statue of Christ is suppose to weigh seven tons and the cross made of redwood is fifty five feet high and weighs fourteen tons."

"We can go to Mass there," Margaret suggested.

"It's almost to the Mackinac Bridge," I said. "And maybe we can make a side trip to see the bridge."

"Where's the bridge," Marty asked.

"It's about three hundred miles from here straight north," I said. "It connects the Lower Peninsula to the Upper Peninsula at St. Ignace. The bridge is five miles long and it is alleged to be the longest suspension bridge in the world."

"Boy, I'd sure like to see that," Robert said.

"Well, we can all see the bridge and some of the Upper Peninsula when we make a day trip from our home base at Burt Lake," I suggested.

"You mean we can cross the five-mile bridge?" Sue asked.

"Yes, it's just a short drive from Burt Lake. We can visit St. Ignace, one of the oldest cities in Michigan," I added. "It's where the founder Father Marquette is buried."

"There's a statue of Father Marquette at the entrance to Belle Isle right here in Detroit," Doc said.

Vacations

The planning for our first family northern vacation continued. We knew the destination and the cost. We were busy planning what kind of luggage we would need to transport nineteen people to the two cottages.

"None of the children except Doc and Bob has any luggage," Delores said.

"Now, that's a problem. Maybe we can use cardboard boxes."

"That's a good idea," everyone chimed in.

"But, they have to be the right size. Not too big and not too small. We will not have room for big boxes. We can use roof racks on the two station wagons, but how many boxes can we tie on each rack?"

"I've got an idea," Tim said. "We can go to Lou's Party Store on Charlevoix and see what kind of boxes he has."

Beer Cases

The next day at the dinner table, Tim reported that Lou suggested that we use empty beer cases. He said that he would loan us seventeen empty beer cases for our trip and we can bring them back when we return. They were clean and just the right size and would be easy to tie them to the racks. Everyone would have an empty beer case for his or her clothes.

"That's a great idea," I said. "Why didn't I think of that? They're the right size and shape and sturdy enough for the trip. They'll be easy to tie to the racks. Can you imagine seventeen beer cases on the roof of our two station wagons? What a sight."

"I wonder what our neighbors are going to say when they see us leaving with all those beer cases," Delores said.

"I can hear them now," Doc said. "There goes Delores and George. I guess their family really like beer."

"What the neighbors say is the least of our problems," I said. "Besides, I'm sure the grapevine will keep every neighbor informed with the correct information."

Driving North

Early in the morning of the day of departure, two station wagons left 1000 Devonshire heading for the Michigan North Country. Delores and I had our station wagons loaded with luggage and children. Delores had all the eight girls and Doc, our seventeen-year-old boy, who would help her drive. I had the remaining eight boys in my station wagon. Seventeen beer cartons were neatly stacked on the top luggage carriers of both cars. Everyone had their own box with their name stuck on the top. All those beer cases on top of two cars were a sight to see.

We had driven for about three hours and I wondered why Delores seemed to have a problem keeping up. I kept slowing down to let her catch up with us. Finally, I signaled for her to follow me at the next rest stop area. When we stopped, I told Delores that she was driving too slowly.

"Delores, "you're not keeping up with me. You're only going about forty miles an hour. Can't you go any faster? We should be doing the speed limit of fifty five mile per hour if we ever want to get there."

"I'm sorry," she said. "I'm going as fast as the car will go. I've got my foot all the way down on the gas pedal."

"Well, OK," I said. "But, look why don't you let Doc take the wheel until the next rest stop. We still have another four hours of driving ahead of us."

"Good idea," she said as she went around to the passenger side of the car.

"Sure. I'll be glad to drive," Doc said.

"You and your mother take turns driving," I said. "Every couple of hours at a rest stop area you can change off."

As I pulled out of the rest stop area and merged into the traffic, I began to accelerate up to fifty mile per hour. I kept my eye on Delores' station wagon with Doc driving to see if they could keep up with me. Looking into the rearview mirror, I saw Doc right behind me. Whatever was wrong with the car seems to be all right now, I thought. Doc was right behind me when we pulled up to a stop at the next rest stop area.

"The car must have fixed itself," I said as I approach Delores' car.

"Yes. It works fine," Doc said. I had no trouble keeping up with you. I could have even gone faster if I wanted to."

"I don't know what the matter was," Delores said.

"Doc, how tall are you?" I asked.

"Oh, about five ten, I guess. Why?"

"And, Delores," I said ignoring his question for the moment. "How tall are you?"

"About five two."

"Did either of you change the seat positions?"

"No."

"Delores, you're eight inches shorter than Doc. Do you think that maybe your foot was not reaching the floorboard? You were extending your foot all the way but it may not have been to the floorboard. When you pushed all the way down on the gas pedal, you may not have been far enough down so forty-five miles per hour was all you could reach. This time when you take over from Doc, move the seat forward so that you're sure that you can reach the floorboard and I'll bet your car will go faster."

"Well, I'll be," Delores, said. "By George, I think you've got it. I purposely did not move the seat forward when I started driving because I knew Doc would be driving and he needs more legroom with his long legs. I think you've solved the problem, George. Let's see if I can keep up with you now."

That was the end to the slow-car problem. Delores moved the seat forward and from then on, she had no problem keeping up.

Burt Lake

The cottage was just as promised. Six bedrooms would accommodate all the girls, the boys, Delores and me very nicely. A beautiful beach was right in front of the cottage. The water was beautiful. You could walk out quite a way before you got to five feet of water. This was great for the children. The evenings were cool, so we made a fire in the fireplace every evening.

After a few days, the owners came by the cottage with a saddled pony.

"We thought the children would enjoy a pony ride," they said.

"They sure would," I agreed. "Most of them have never been on a real live pony.

"Great, horseback riding," Bob, said. "I'll get the movie camera. We've got to have this on film."

"Good idea," I said. "Everyone can take a turn riding the pony and we'll take pictures of each one of you just like the old western round up of cowboys and cowgirls riding on the range."

Everyone rode the pony, including me. Tim and Joe were able to gallop a little way but when I tried riding the pony, he must have thought that I was too heavy and the pony tried to scrape me off by rubbing me up against a tree. Smart pony!

All in all, all had a fun time and the pony ride was great for the children.

"I hear that you all went to see the Mackinac Straits Bridge," the owner's wife said. "How did you like the trip?" speaking to Janet Arsenault, one of our four-year olds.

"Fine, thank you," Janet answered.

"And you," pointing to four-year-old little Mary Ann McMillan, "what did you see on your trip?"

"We saw where one of daddy's friends is buried," she answered.

We all laughed. "She's referring to the Father Marquette's National Memorial grave site at St. Ignace," I said. "I guessed she thought that Father Marquette was a friend of mine because of all the fuss I made about his burial site."

Poison Ivy

"Dad, I've got an itch and a rash all over my legs," Bob said to me showing me his red skinned legs.

"Were you walking bare legged in the weeds?"

"Well, there's a bunch of weeds around where I pulled the boat up from the beach."

"It looks like a case of poison ivy. Tell everyone to stay out of the weeds. Pass the word around. Meanwhile, see your mother and have her put some lotion on it. Try not to scratch it."

Outside of poison ivy and a few other minor problems, everyone in the family had a great time swimming, fishing and touring on our first vacation as a family. We would have extended it another week, but the owners said that they were expecting some of their family and they would not be able to rent us another week. I secretly think that although the owners liked having us there, the septic tanks would not take another week of nineteen people flushing the two toilets. We had been told by the owner not to flush all the time. I never realized that septic tanks could fill up and overflow.

The summer vacation up north was great fun and all agreed that we should do it again the following year. All went well on our drive back to 1000 Devonshire and we all arrived safe and sound with our seventeen beer cases on top of the cars and none the worse after being away only one week. *Be it ever so humble, there's no place like home.*

Lake Huron

The following summer, we made plans to rent the same Burt Lake cottage again. But, it was not available. However, we were able to rent a cottage right on Lake Huron a few miles south of Alpena where the water temperature in July never gets any warmer than sixty degrees.

Not many wanted to go swimming that year. We felt that it was important for all to go swimming at least once on every summer vacation. So, that summer was born the new *Polar Bear Club.* All were invited to be members. The initiation consisted of swimming in the beautiful Lake Huron waters. Preparation included taking 8mm movies of the event. The initiation ceremonies for the inductees would be a joint swim for all the new *Polar Bears* as they were made members of this exclusive club. Delores was ready with the movie camera to properly record the great event. We were all lined up on the beach and when I counted to three, we would all run into the water and dive in headfirst. All, including me, agreed to this method of initiation. As we all ran into the water we were to shout *Polar Bear* as we all dived in headfirst.

The theory and hypothesized was: the body heat would last for several minutes and if you could jump in and out right away, you wouldn't feel the cold and you would become an honored member of the *Polar Bears.*

Simple. All were ready when the count went to *one, two, three go!* All in the line went running for the water as a long line of runners. All dove into the water except one ... Patrick. As we looked back, Patrick, one of our twelve year olds, had, at the last minute, stopped short and was standing high and dry on the beach laughing. There was an immediate agreement by all that Patrick would join the *Polar Bears* and become a member in good standing. Needless to say, as a large group of brothers and sisters turned to assist Patrick, he jumped into the water and diving head first, he became a member of the great *Polar Bear Club*. He was duly given membership into this select and elite group.

Our family vacation was wonderful and all the way home, we sang, *Hail, Hail, The Gangs All Here, Freckles Was His Name,* and *There's A Hole In The Bottom Of The Sea.*

XVII

HOLIDAYS

The luxury of doing for others surpasses every other personal enjoyment.

John Gay 1685-1732.

"What costume can I wear for Halloween?" was a question coming from each of the children as the last day of October came around.

"Use your imagination and dress up as something," Delores said.

"That's right. The best costumes are right from your imagination," I said in agreement.

That settled the issue. The children and Delores created costumes and disguises for Halloween. Delores had designed and made a costume of a rabbit for the previous Easter. This rabbit costume was one that was ready for use when Halloween came around. This was the time of year when strange characters would suddenly take form. It was a challenge for all the children to make their own costumes. The rabbit costume was especially successful and appeared year after year with different people in it. Delores was the first to appear as the rabbit. Later, anybody who was near five feet tall would take over the costume.

After Halloween, came Thanksgiving, another memorable time. The entire family would participate in the Thanksgiving Day decorations in preparation of the big family turkey dinner. Delores' father and mother, grandparents, and my mother would attend with some of uncles and aunts. They would all bring something for the dinner. It was nothing to seat thirty-five or forty for dinner with all the trimmings. Usually we had two turkeys and a large ham buffet style. I would carve the two turkeys and I would also slice the ham with my super butcher type meat-slicer.

Before Thanksgiving could cool down, we were busy making plans for Christmas. This was the most anticipated holiday of all. It would start with the family going to a tree farm to look for the *right* Christmas tree. We needed one about eighteen-feet for the center hall entrance because the main staircase would go up about ten steps to a large landing that would turn for about six feet and then continue up another five steps. There was a large hammered brass center chandelier hanging from the ceiling of the second floor down to just above the first floor. This area was perfect for the Christmas tree.

At the tree farm, we would look for the biggest tree and it had to be a thin tree so as to not be too heavy. But we needed a full tree that would look nice.

"That tree is too small," big Mary Ann said as we looked at a Scotch pine in the grove.

"Here's one that's really big," Robert shouted from across the way.

Everyone ran over to check out Robert's big tree. All agreed that this tree would reach up to the second floor of our stairway hall entrance. The tree farmer said that it would cost five dollars a foot and the tree we had picked was about seventeen feet.

"There's that number again!" Marty said.

"We'll take it," I said, "if we can tie it up to the rack on my station wagon.

"Sure. We'll help you," he said.

"If a little is good, bigger is better," Tim said.

"Are you sure it's safe to carry this home?" Delores asked.

"Leave that to me," I said. "We have fifty feet of rope to tie it up with and we have plenty of able bodied man power to help put it on the roof and take it off. We'll just take our time going home and stay off the expressway.

"Well, George, I hope you know what you're doing," Delores said.

"Trust me," I said as I went around to start cutting the tree down.

"We'll hold it up," Joe said as he held on to some branches.

"No. Stand back everyone and let the tree fall in the clearing to the right."

I went to the right and cut a V-shaped notch. Then I went behind the notch and began to cut towards the notch.

"Here she comes!" Patrick shouted.

"Timber!" I yelled, just for the effect, as the tree slowly bent over and fell to the ground right where we wanted it to fall. All available hands picked it up and we carried it over to the car and placed it on the top roof rack. The tree extended a little over the hood of the car and over the trunk. We tied a red flag on it for safety. The trip back home was a happy ride, which included a stop at McDonald's for hot chocolate and hamburgers. It was the usual order of seventeen hamburgers and seventeen hot chocolates. The clerk, who took the order, asked me to repeat it twice more. Then she called her manager who filled the order.

Our first Christmas tree in the new house was perfect. It reached up to the second floor in the entrance hallway staircase.

With the new tree stand, it reached up about eighteen feet. Getting the tree through the front door was a task that took a little patience. "Easy does it," I said as the boys and I carried it through the large oak door.

The decorations started a little at a time. Everyone did his or her part. We would walk up the stairway and hang decorations and lights reaching over the banister all the way up to the second floor.

The older boys used a ladder to decorate the other side. By the end of the week the tree was mostly decorated. There was always something that someone wanted to add to the tree. But, when all the lights were up and turned on, it lit up the downstairs and the second floor hallway. Tall Christmas trees became the tradition for the front hall stairway. It was the focal point for all the festivities of a joyful season that lasted the month of December. Presents for the grandparents and a few others were placed under the tree and added color to the decorations. But, the best presents, the ones from *Santa Claus,* would be hidden and never be seen until Christmas morning. The Christmas tree decorating effort was never really complete until the nineteen Christmas stockings were hung on the banister all the way up the front staircase. Delores made sure that everyone had a Christmas stocking with his or her name on it

Children up the stairway

"When is Santa Claus coming?" little Mary Ann asked.

"On Christmas Eve when everyone is sleeping." Delores. said.

"I don't believe that," Marty said.

"Only those who believe, receive."

"Oh, I believe," Marty, said. "I really believe." And a whole chorus of "I believe" went up from everybody.

"So do I," Delores said.

"We'll all go to Midnight Mass and after Mass, we can have a light snack and off to bed so Santa Claus can come with the presents," I said thinking of the job ahead for Delores and me.

"Whoever wakes up first, wake me up," Marty said not wishing to miss out on Christmas morning.

"Me too," a chorus replied.

Christmas

How do the parents of seventeen children decide who gets what and how much? Delores devised a method to do just that in an equitable manner. She put a Santa Claus list of all the names on the family bulletin board and it was up to the children to place their orders to Santa Claus. The necessary sizes and colors would also be noted. Santa Claus had said that he would try to get at least two of the items for everybody. The Santa Clause list went up when the Christmas tree went up. So, there was always plenty of time for the children to make up their minds. Santa was especially good at filling orders for clothes. But, a few toys and games were among the many items from Santa. There was a toy room in the basement reserved for all the games and toys accumulated from seventeen children. Each Christmas would add to our collection.

Delores and I decided that the recreation room in the basement would be the room where Santa Claus would leave the presents on Christmas morning. It was a ballroom with hardwood flooring and a fireplace. This would spare the upstairs and make it easier to keep neat. The basement recreation room was a very nice room. As I had mentioned before, there was a small 'bar room' attached to the recreation room with a lock on the door. This room was always locked before Christmas because that was where Santa Claus would store all the presents until Christmas morning.

At 5 a.m., Christmas morning, Delores and I had finally finished setting up all the presents. We had been up all night, having gone to Midnight Mass and then working to get everything ready after the last one went to bed. This was the children's first Christmas in the new house.

"We might as well stay up now," I said to Delores as we put the finishing touches on our work.

"It's all right with me. We can catch some sleep later."

"Maybe," I said. As I set up the movie camera on tri-pods to record the happy event. What a momentous occasion. This was to be our first Christmas with our seventeen children.

All we had to do was go upstairs and knock on big Mary Ann and Tish's bedroom door to wake them up and the rest is will be history. I expected the excitement to go through the house like wild fire. But, as they slowly came down the stairs, after about only four hours sleep, in their pajamas and bathrobes, wiping sleep from their eyes, I was recording this with my movie camera.

"Hold it. That won't do," I said as I stopped the camera. "Everyone back! That's no way to enter Santa Claus's room on Christmas morning. Everyone back out and come back in excited. This time, show some feeling, joy and happiness for the movie camera. Look surprised. Now when I count three come back in with some enthusiasm."

Out they all went and I reset the camera to 'on'. "One, two, three come on in now!" I shouted.

They were all good actors. I recorded their "surprised" looks and excitement. The presents were passed around until they found the person with their name on it. After a few hours, they took their treasures up to their rooms and went back to bed to catch up on some much needed sleep.

After Christmas, the whole family hated to take down the Christmas tree. As long as it held its beauty and the needles didn't shed too badly, we would leave it up. That first year, the tree stayed up until February. One year, the neighborhood talk was, that spring was not far away, the Arsenault/McMillans finally threw out their Christmas tree.

Easter

Easter time was another annual family event. We always had an Easter party and the rabbit costume was taken out for the occasion. The Easter Bunny would show up on Easter morning to start the festivities when the family would gather around to start the traditional Easter Hunt. As part of the hunt, children had to find their Easter basket, which had their name on it. There were nineteen baskets hidden all around the house. Many were behind doors and in closets. If you found a basket and it didn't have your name on it, you just left it and continued to look for your own basket. Some baskets were in some very unusual places. And some baskets were nowhere to be found. I suspected that some baskets were changed from place to place so the owner had to keep looking not realizing that it might be where he had already looked. When you found your own basket, then the fun was to continue to look for those who had not found their basket just so you would know ahead of them where it was hidden. Then you would watch them searching for it. As I said, the last one would sometimes be changed to different hiding places two or three times. This alleged conspiracy was said to be among the older children having fun changing the hiding place of the basket just in the nick of time. However, this alleged conspiracy was never proven.

All in all, the holidays provided a time when all the family would enjoy the festivities. Whenever the family congregated, they enjoyed each other's company and there were always enough people to have a party and it's still like that today.

XVIII

TAXES

> *The worth of a state, in the long run, is the worth of the individuals composing it.*
>
> John S. Mill 1806-1873

The world is filled with good guys and bad guys and every one of us has a little good and evil somewhere inside. The task is to accentuate the good and eliminate the bad. Seems simple enough. Somebody said, *there's a little bit of bad in the best of us and a little bit of good in the worst of us, so it ill behooves any of us to talk about the rest of us.* This thesis has been around for a long time and holds true in all walks of life and even in governments. Fate has a way of surprising us with the unexpected whenever we find life getting dull. For example, in September, a few years after we were married, I received a letter from the Internal Revenue Service of the United States government, which included this statement.

> *In examining your Federal Income Tax return for*
> *The above year, we find that we need additional*
> *Information from your records to determine your*
> *Tax liability. We have arranged an appointment*
> *As we have shown above. Under the law, taxpayers are re-*
> *Required on request to substantiate all expenses and*
> *Deductions.*

"Here we go," I said to Delores. "The IRS doesn't believe we have seventeen children. I just knew this would happen."

"What do you mean, they don't believe us?" Delores said. "You just go down there and tell them they can come to our house and see for themselves."

"Oh, I know. But, you can't just go down there and tell them to come and see for themselves. They want evidence. When the IRS wants to see your records for expenses, they usually want to look at everything. We'll just have to go down there and take all my records with us and also we'll take a copy of the front page of the Detroit News article on our marriage as evidence."

"What do you mean, we?" Delores said. "Well, you're an accountant. You don't need me. I'm not worried. I'm sure you can handle this all by yourself. You have all the evidence that you'll need."

"Easier said than done Delores. In the first place, anyone can make a mistake, even accountants although, I'm pretty sure I didn't make any mistakes. It must be the number of dependents changed from last year that they want to check. And, while they're checking my dependents, they probably think, they might as well check everything."

"Well, just do the best you can dear," Delores said. "Besides, if they put you in jail, think of all the mail you'll get from the children."

"Thanks, Delores. Remember, you signed that tax return too. So, maybe we should go down to the IRS together. That way, if we both go to jail, we'll both be getting a lot of letters from the children."

"No sir. That's your job. But don't worry about it, George," Delores said. "Remember, the IRS is made up of people just like you and me trying to make a living … just ordinary people. You go down there and straighten them out and that will be the end of that. I know you can do it."

"I hope so," I said.

Really, I thought, I shouldn't have to worry. I have nothing to hide. If I made a mistake, so be it. I'll just correct it and pay them the difference. Anyone can make a mistake on these complicated income tax returns. I'm only human. They still sell pencils with erasers on them. The only person who can't make a mistake on his income tax is the guy who doesn't submit one and that's a bigger mistake. All I need to do is take all my canceled checks and pay stubs with all my receipts and me and records that I used to fill in my tax return plus my copy of the return. The big photo on the front page of the Detroit News should be all the evidence they need of my new status as a father of seventeen children and a new wife. All the names are in the story so why should I worry. I always thought that they might not believe this anyway. Sooner or later, they were bound to ask questions and it might as well be now and get it over with.

After the forgoing analysis and processing in my mind, I felt better about the IRS inquiry. I was sure that I had covered all the bases and I was ready for my appointment.

The IRS

The day was cloudy when I entered the U.S. Federal Building in downtown Detroit. The reckoning with the IRS had arrived. The receptionist directed me down the hall to room 201.

Mr. IRS Examiner was waiting for me and he greeted me at the door. "Come right in, Mr. Arsenault," he said as I entered. The receptionist must have called him and told him I was coming, I thought. He closed the door behind me.

"Have a seat," he said, and went behind his desk.

Come into my parlor, said the spider to the fly. I thought.

"I see that you brought your records," he said, pointing to my briefcase.

"Yes! I didn't know exactly what you wanted, so I brought everything that I could think of that would help straighten this mess up," I said, opening my briefcase and taking out some of the papers.

"Did you bring all the birth certificates for your seventeen children?"

"Birth certificates?" I said. "Well. No. I'm not even sure we could find birth certificates for all seventeen children. I didn't realize the you would want birth certificates."

"Well, that's your best evidence of the children that you claim as dependents."

"As I said, I don't even know if we have birth certificates for all seventeen children. I know I haven't seen any of the McMillan children's certificates. I'm pretty sure that we have all the baptismal certificates but I'll bet we don't have all the birth certificates. I guess I could get them from the city records for a fee, right?"

"Right!" he said. "The baptismal certificates would help, but I guess that you didn't bring those either, right?"

"Right," I said. "That's where I slipped up. I never thought that you would want them."

"Well, we will need some evidence that the seventeen children are really your dependents."

"Here is the front page of The Detroit News for the day after we were married," I said pulling out the paper and hastily handing him the paper from my briefcase. "That could be used as evidence. Can't it?"

"Hmm," he said, as he carefully began reading the story. Looking up he said, "So you're the guy with seven children that married the widow with ten children from Grosse Pointe."

"Yes, I'm the guy," I said, emphatically as he kept reading.

When he finished reading the whole story, he said, "I remember reading this a couple of years ago. I told my wife, "Here's a couple not afraid to raise a large family in this day and age."

"Well, we're doing our best, and I think we're winning,"

He got up and said, "I'll be right back," as he walk to the door with the newspaper clipping in his hand. When he returned in a few minutes, he said, "I'm giving you a clearance on all your tax returns up to this date. You won't have us bothering you for a long time."

"You both deserve a lot of credit. God bless you. I think that anyone raising that many children shouldn't have to pay any taxes at all."

"Thank you very much." Boy, I thought, I've got the right guy this time.

"I'll take a quick look at the rest of your records, but I'm sure that everything else is all right. Do you mind if I keep this newspaper clipping for our records?"

"By all means. You're welcome to them. I brought them especially for you.   Thank you very much," I said as I put my records back into my briefcase.   Man, did I come to the right place, I thought, as I was leaving the building. Now, there's a smart man. First order of business when I get home … get birth certificates for all seventeen children. Note: the IRS never asked about my dependents again.

XIX

The Final Analysis

> *Nothing is nobler; nothing is more venerable than fidelity.*
>
> *Faithfulness and truth are the most sacred Excellencies*
>
> *They are the endowments of the human mind.*
>
> Marcus Cicero-106-43 BC

The marriage was a huge success because all nineteen contributed to our magnificent venture. All seventeen children made their own contributions with their best foot forward from the very day we began to plan this union. It was because of each one's total commitment to the family with each doing their part that the venture worked so well. It has been my experience that when more than one agree on a goal, that goal is more attainable by the multiple of those that agree. Thus the *multiple progressions phenomenal* were one of our strong points. It's like the tide in the ocean. *Once the tide starts to come in, there's no way you can hold it back.*

For example, Delores and I were "mom and dad to all the children." This decision came right from the children in the very beginning of our marriage. The older boys had come to me and asked me what I wanted to be called: George, Mr. Arsenault, father, dad?

I said, "Call me whatever you are comfortable with."

They went out and in a few minutes, they came back and said, "We've decided to call you *dad.*"

And it's been *dad* ever since. That was a vote of confidence for me. I knew they were all smart children. They had realized the value of our objective goals we had set for our union. Once the commitment was made in good faith, we did not waiver from our goal. The rest was easy. "I am as constant as the Northern Star," *Caesar* had said. And, so were we. We were firm on our mission.

"Will God with our petitions in prayer help us to succeed?" That was another question in our minds. If God is almighty, then it follows that He can do anything. Therefore, if we could get God in our corner, we'd be sure to succeed. However, I realize that God makes no *special deals*. You can't say to God, "If you do this for me, I'll do this for you." Sorry, no deal. The answer is as I've said before: Work as if everything depended on you and pray as if everything depended on God.

So, what was the answer? Like Thomas Edison once said, "*genius is just plain hard work*." The success of our marriage, or any marriage for that matter, is *just plain hard work*. However, I would grant that one must start out with good raw material. We had good raw material, seventeen great children. I told Delores that someday there will be seventeen shining jewels in her crown when she gets to heaven.

Years ago, I read an axiom, "eagles don't see flies." This always stuck with me. Eagles are so majestic that they are not concerned with flies. It meant to me that one should not let little things bother them. It meant that I should aim high and not let little things upset me.

One of Delores' many talents was ceramics and she was aware of my fascination for the flying wing spread eagle. She made me a *wing spread eagle*. Not one that sits on a ledge, but one that was in flight, and I used this as a symbol of our family. My philosophy was to be majestic enough to overlook small mistakes and overlook the small troubles of life and keep your eye on the sky and fly high enough to see the big picture. Another analogy I made involved lighthouses. Lighthouses are beacons in the night for aid to those that are lost and I've tried to be a beacon for our children, hoping to show them the safe way. Delores also made me a ceramic lighthouse for my desk.

If I learned anything in this endeavor of raising seventeen children, it was this:

Children are little individuals ... real people ... very important people and very special people with all the talent and potential for being good. Delores and I saw us as the children's teachers, coaches, and guides. We did not do our jobs as disciplinarians but rather as teachers. We were not enforcers of statutory laws with punishment. We believed that violence begets violence and love begets love. Therefore, violent discipline as punishment actually teaches the child that it is permissible for big people to hurt small people. This may be the reason that there is so much violence in the world. The wrong lesson is being taught to our youth. When behavior needs correcting, we learned to use other methods and strategies to alter a child's behavior rather then physical punishment. The old adage "spare the rod and spoil the child," in our mind, is wrong. For example, a non-violent consequence could be "go to your room," or "go stand in the corner," depending on age. The word *grounded* was well understood by my teenagers. "You're grounded for a week," was a sentence to be avoided. This was the non-violent discipline preferred.

Behavior modification starts by giving the children a good self-image. "Our children are all good children," was a statement often heard by our friends and neighbors from Delores and me. When children hear this being said to others, they have a reputation to live up to. If they were told that they were bad, then what's to stop them from saying, "I'm bad anyhow, so what!" Not a good image to live up to. The old axiom, *give a man a good reputation and he may try to live up to it.* I believe it was St. Augustine who once said, *you may not be a saint, but if you act like one, maybe you will become one.*

Murray A. Straus, a sociologist from the University of New Hampshire, concluded after his group research on child behavior, that spanking was linked to later anti-social behavior despite social economics, status, or ethnic background, parenting style, emotional warmth and other factors. Thus, corporal punishment, which includes spanking, does not promote good social adults in society. Antisocial behavior like cheating, stealing, lying, being mean to others, breaking things and defiance in the home and in school, trouble getting along with others, may be linked to corporal punishment at an early age. Delores' thesis was that children need to be loved and the earlier the better is true. Like a puppy dog, they will love you back. They see the world through the parent's example. I always agree adamantly with Delores.

It has always been my opinion that what everyone really needs is wise and benevolent counseling. We would have all benefited from this type of learning. While Delores and I may be lacking in wisdom as parents, we asserted that our loving benevolence was boundless. We love them all very much for all the happiness they have given us all these years. The secret of a teacher is that sometimes the teacher also learns many things along with the student. So it was with us.

So if we've gained any wisdom in our journey as parents of seventeen, we wish to leave it for them in this book. As time goes on, every one of us tend to forget all the happenings and events that made us a large happy family. Time and memory make it difficult to remember and convey the lessons we learned on our way to future generations. Therefore, this book is not only a history of events but also all the counseling and problem solutions that Delores and I were able to convey for their edification and practice so that they too can instruct and improve their lives spiritually, morally, and materially and those that follow. But most important, we must *keep the faith.* I've been known to say, "if it was good enough for my father, it good enough for me." And as Patrick Henry so aptly put it in his writings:

I have now disposed of all of my property to my family. There is one thing more that I wish I could give them, and that is the Christian religion. If they had that and I had not given them one shilling, they would have been rich, and if they had not that, and I had given them the entire world, they would be poor. Patrick Henry—(1736-1799)

My family motto: "Garder la Foi"

Our daughter Aileen Arsenault wrote this following poem in 1991 on our 25th Wedding Anniversary.

THE FAMILY
By
Aileen T. Arsenault

The story begins,
As they most often do;
With a man and a woman,
Starting anew ...
She with her ten,
And he with his seven;
Decided to wed,
And create their own heaven.

And who would have known,
On that clear day in June,
How two families could become one,
And not a moment too soon.

The two youngest were age three,
The oldest boy seventeen;
Six girls and eight boys,
Filled the range in between.

Though not always easy;
Or fully understood;
The joining of families,
Brought bounties of good.

Our blessings have been many,
Our sorrows soften by love.

As bonds of our family have deepened,
With help from Mark up above.

And so we come together,
To celebrate this day;
All one, though many,
Each in our own special way.

ABOUT THE AUTHOR

H. George Arsenault is a retired General Motors Senior Financial Analyst and Financial data base programmer with 36 years service and seven years with a Chrysler subsidiary, VPSI, as a Systems Information Director. He now lives with his wife, Delores, in St. Clair Shores, Michigan.

H. George Arsenault has three Degrees:
Bachelor of Commercial Science in Finance
Bachelor of Science in Management
Master of Arts in Public Administration

978-0-595-45597-3
0-595-45597-2

CPSIA information can be obtained at www.ICGtesting.com
Printed in the USA
LVOW07s0613110915

453537LV00001B/1/P